23-11-94.

DEAR ALMA.

WELCOME HOME.

GOD BLESS ALWAYS

JOAN BISHOP

THE RELIGIOUS SMUTS

THE RELIGIOUS SMUTS

Piet Beukes

HUMAN & ROUSSEAU
Cape Town   Johannesburg

Contents

Introduction

The great statesman and military leader Jan Christiaan Smuts, described in my first two books, *The Holistic Smuts* and *The Romantic Smuts*, was also a deeply religious man, a devoted Christian and an admirer and follower of Jesus.

Unfortunately, many people who did not know Smuts personally and who did not agree with his politics and statecraft regarded him as irreligious and criticised him for this.

Some went even further and saw him as an agnostic who embraced atheism. Especially after the appearance of his book *Holism and Evolution* in 1926, most of his detractors were convinced that he was not only a materialist but a confirmed atheist. This was because he accepted the German philosopher Kant's doctrine that from the facts of nature no inference to a transcendent mind – in other words a God – is justified.

Even his intellectual friend, the eminent Monsignor Dr F. C. Kolbe, who had converted from Protestantism to Roman Catholicism, attacked Smuts in a series of private papers for accepting Kant's "blunder", as he called it. For him, as for many religious people, man discovers God through His Creation.

There were also those who objected to Smuts's ready acceptance of Charles Darwin's theory of evolution which was, and still is in the minds of some, regarded as a denial of God's Creation.

Smuts seldom defended himself publicly. Privately he stated that he was prepared to leave the final verdict on his life and views to posterity. But in his private letters, especially to Margaret Clark Gillett, whom he regarded as his closest friend and to whom he wrote some 2 000 letters, there is seldom one in which he does not discuss or at least mention religion.

There are also his various public addresses in which he publicly confessed his religion, his belief in God, his acceptance of Jesus Christ, his admiration of the Jews as the authors of the Bible and his various personal experiences of the Spirit of God in his own life.

In my first book, *The Holistic Smuts: A Study in Personality*, I devoted a full chapter to his religion, revealing how he embraced the Christian religion from his earliest youth on a farm in South Africa until his dying day 80 years later.

In all my research which covers his entire life I have not discovered any incident at any time or place where he was assailed by doubts as to the veracity of his religion. Smuts was a firm believer in God as the Father and Creator of the Universe and he accepted Jesus Christ as his Saviour.

He stated this clearly in his address in August 1934 on the Bible.

"As history the Bible embodies the whole story of mankind. It is a record extending thousands of years into the past – a record which has been confirmed by and filled out by researchers of science. There is the Bible of prophecy, with its fine ethical ideals pointing the way to all mankind. It is an interpretation of life, filling out the Greek conception that the pursuit of reason is the way of truth. The Bible does not look upon the Universe as a world of reason, but more as a world of mystery, a divine world.

"I cannot say which is the correct interpretation of life, but I suggest that the two have to be taken together.

"On the one hand, the Greek ideal of being faithful to the light of the mind, and on the other hand the Biblical conception of faith. Indeed it seems to me that the Jew probably read deeper and saw deeper into the meaning of life than the Greek. There are depths in the human soul that the mind will probably never fathom and the ultimate interpretation of life may be found through a combination of Plato and Paul. The word has also been interpreted as power, in the light of the immensity of nature.

"In our pursuit of power as nations, we have made havoc of the world. In our pursuit of national greatness, we have trodden underfoot many great ideals of the human race. As against this pursuit of power we have the Biblical view of life, of life as love, as tenderness and as mercy.

"It is this aspect of the Bible that made Nietzsche call Christianity a

8

slave religion, but the so-called slave virtues represent the highest ideals of the human race. The man who saw that, saw further into the nature of the universe. That is why we made him a God.

"My own belief is that we have in the Bible insights into truth, beauty and goodness, and into the ultimate human ideal, which are not mere fashion, but which are immortal and eternal," he concluded.

As someone who knew Smuts personally during the last twelve years of his life and worked closely with him, first during the Second World War and later as the editor in chief of his various political newspapers, I can state categorically that he was deeply religious and saw and experienced the hand of God in his own life and in the destiny of mankind as a whole. The Bible and especially the New Testament in the original Greek language were his constant companions together with a variety of scientific and philosophical books. Wherever he went the small Greek New Testament could be found on his bedside table.

Even his wife Isie learnt to read the New Testament in Greek, and one day surprised her husband by reciting the entire chapter 13 of 1 Corinthians on love in Greek. Smuts was surprised and amused but also proud of his brilliant wife and told his friends and visitors about it.

In the original Greek version the word for love is given as *agape*, but in a broader sense it also refers to brotherly love and to charity. In the English translation of the New Testament the word "charity" is used, but in Afrikaans and Dutch the word *liefde* and in German versions the word *Liebe* is used to translate the Greek word. Smuts in one of his letters explained that the Greek word *agape* has a wide meaning, covering both sensuous and brotherly love, as well as charity.

Let me mention an instance where I personally experienced his acceptance of the hand of God in our lives. It occurred in Parliament in Cape Town in 1949. One of the ministers in his Cabinet when he was prime minister, Mr J. W. Mushet, invited a few personal friends to lunch in the dining room in Parliament to introduce a visiting Australian professor of Political Science to General Smuts, who was then the Leader of the Opposition. My wife and I were also included as at the time I was the editor in chief of five newspapers which supported Smuts and his United Party. My wife sat next to Smuts and I was seated opposite him and next to the Australian professor. Also present was a South African housewife and her husband. She looked extremely depressed.

The conversation was lively and elevated right from the start of the lunch. Smuts and the Australian exchanged views on the fundamental principles of international statecraft. Then the talk switched to life in general.

Suddenly the depressed woman spoke up. "What I would like to know is what is the purpose of life; why do we exist?"

Smuts had a habit of referring to all women as "my child". I waited for it and sure enough it came without any wavering or hesitation.

"My child, you live and you exist to glorify your God who created you, that is the purpose of your life."

And there was also his enduring faith in God and his acceptance of Jesus as his guide and saviour, as I will reveal with chapter and verse, as the saying goes.

CHAPTER ONE

The spirit of the mountain

Smuts's personal religion was based entirely on the Bible and particularly on the New Testament which he preferred to read in the original Greek.

Although he was a member of the Dutch Reformed Church in South Africa, he was not a regular churchgoer but appreciated the work and the values of the Church as an instrument to uplift the minds and the hearts of people in the service of God. But he never liked church dogma and preferred to contemplate and explore in his own mind the inner meaning of religion and the revelations of God and the Holy Spirit in the lives of people and especially in his own life.

I must stress, however, that Smuts never contemplated writing a theological or even a philosophical dissertation on Christianity or even on religion in general, but he was forever searching for and investigating the true meaning of religion and faith in God and especially in Jesus Christ.

What is so remarkable is that in his letters to his special friends he constantly introduced almost at random ideas which welled up within him as he read the Bible. Especially in times of crisis when the fate of individuals or nations, indeed of all humanity, was hanging in the balance, Smuts poured out his soul in brilliant enquiries. This was also the time when his faith in God came to the fore most clearly.

It was especially to Margaret Clark Gillett that he poured out his hopes, his doubts, his anxieties and his desires to find answers to the riddles of life and to the inner meaning of religion.

Smuts and Margaret decided in the year 1919 to write weekly letters to one another. This was at a time when Smuts realised that he would have to return to South Africa permanently after he had lived in England almost continually since the outbreak of the First World War in 1914. England during those years needed his wisdom and his service – Churchill acknowledged this in several letters to him – both in war and peace, while his friend and mentor General Louis Botha looked after the affairs of South Africa. But in 1919 Botha suddenly died and Smuts was chosen as his successor as prime minister. He had to return to South Africa immediately, but before he left England he and Margaret made a pact to write to one another every week if at all possible. Sure enough, once he was back in South Africa the weekly letters kept flowing between them until his death in 1950, although there were times when neither he nor she could keep to the weekly schedule.

At first he also received letters from his romantic friend Alice Clark, Margaret's sister, as well as the third Clark sister, Hilda, who as a medical doctor was performing acts of charity in Austria. Alice was very much in love with Jan Smuts and wrote to him about "Love" and "Truth" and "Life", and the other great "capitals", as he called them. In a letter to her on 21 October 1919 he told her he was immersed in small things and he consoled himself with David Harum's philosophy that "fleas are good for a dog" as it keeps him from brooding over being a dog.

Smuts was not eager to continue his letters to Alice, as he preferred to write to Margaret every week as she to him. He was also over-worked, as most of his ministers were either ill or absent. He himself was also ill, exhausted and despondent. The doctors who saw him told him to take a rest to recover his health.

Unfortunately for him and for the country it was at this time that the mineworkers on the Golden Rand started a general strike. Smuts was forced to hasten to Johannesburg to face the strikers. Here he showed his character as a stern, severe politician and military leader, and when Alice took him to task, he wrote to her on 24 March 1922:

"You will have seen in the papers about the disturbances in the general strike by the mineworkers on the Rand which in the end had to be forcibly quelled. I went up country for the purpose and have added further claims to the title of butcher and hangman."

Smuts tried to justify himself to Alice.

"I could not help it. Throughout I have been influenced by kindly feelings to the workers. But there was madness in their blood, and in the end blood-letting became necessary. It is all bad-luck on the country, and on me personally, but it could not be avoided. The doctors ordered me away for a month's rest at the beginning of December, and instead of a holiday I have been occupied by this sort of situation.

"Do you really think that under those circumstances I could practise your gospel of blind cheerfulness? I believe in the great ideals of life as you know, but I also believe that, as the flowers grow on a granite soil, so life with all its beautiful flowering rests at last on a granite foundation. Unless society is to go to pieces there must be a solid guarantee of force in the background, and this will remain so until human nature has undergone a thorough change."

Smuts was condemned for his brutality to the workers both in Parliament as well as in international circles. He poured out his heart to Margaret. On 20 December 1922 he wrote to her: "You were right. Figs do not grow on thistles. And the Great War of 1914-18 could not be expected to lead to the spiritual salvation of mankind. I had hoped that the great lesson had gone home. But evidently the Great War has taught us nothing but evil so far. And yet some unseen Power may be guiding us through this dark night. If I did not have this last vestige of a faith, I would really not be able to go on.

"Christianity began in the slaves' quarters of the decadent Roman Empire, and so some seed of good may be germinating in the hearts of men."

At the time very few people except his own wife Isie and Margaret and Alice and some other personal friends in England and South Africa knew him as a religious man. He was mostly known and admired or condemned as a stern, uncompromising military leader who was prepared to use force.

Then on 25 February 1923 he climbed Table Mountain to unveil a memorial to members of the Mountain Club who had fallen in the Great War of 1914-18. Shortly after his speech he reported to Margaret that it was a unique occasion and he had made "a little speech which found great favour". He sent her a copy. "It is a bit of me and not merely a speech" was how he described it.

It was not until this great oration on Table Mountain that the people suddenly heard out of his own mouth what a deep interest he took in religion and his full acceptance of the Gospel of Jesus in the Sermon on the Mount.

His speech under the title "The Spirit of the Mountain" was compared to the historic oration of the Athenian statesman Pericles in the fifth century B.C. as well as with Abraham Lincoln's famous address at Gettysburg. It was given at Maclear's Beacon on Table Mountain.

"The Mountain is not merely something externally sublime. It has a great historical and spiritual meaning for us. It stands for us as the ladder of life. Nay, more, it is the great ladder of the soul, and in a curious way the source of religion. From it came the Law, from it came the Gospel in the Sermon on the Mount. We may truly say that the highest religion is the Religion of the Mountain.

"What is that religion? When we reach the mountain summits we leave behind us all the things that weigh heavily down below on our body and our spirit. We leave behind a feeling of weakness and depression; we feel a new freedom, a great exhilaration, an exaltation of the body no less than of the spirit. We feel a great joy.

"The Religion of the Mountain is in reality the religion of joy, of the release of the soul from the things that weigh it down and fill it with a sense of weariness, sorrow and defeat. The religion of joy realises the freedom of the soul, the soul's kinship to the great creative spirit, and its dominance over all the things of sense. As the body has escaped from the over-weight and depression of the sea, so the soul must be released from all sense of weariness, weakness and depression arising from the fret, worry and friction of our daily lives. We must feel that we are above it all, that the soul is essentially free, and in freedom realises the joy of living. And when the feeling of lassitude and depression and the sense of defeat advances upon us, we must repel it, and maintain an equal and cheerful temper.

"We must fill our daily lives with the spirit of joy and delight. We must carry this spirit into our daily lives and tasks. We must perform our work not grudgingly and as a burden imposed upon us, but in a spirit of cheerfulness, goodwill and delight in it. Not only on the mountain summits of life, not only on the heights of success and achievement, but down in the deep valleys of drudgery, of anxiety and defeat, we must cultivate this great spirit of joyous freedom and upliftment of the soul.

"We must practise the Religion of the Mountain down in the valleys also.

"This may sound a hard doctrine, and it may be that only after years

14

of practice are we able to triumph in spirit over the things that weigh and drag us down. But it is the nature of the soul, as of all life, to rise, to overcome, and finally to attain complete freedom and happiness. And if we consistently practise the Religion of the Mountain we must succeed in the end. To this great end Nature will co-operate with the soul.

"The mountains uphold us and the stars beckon to us. The mountains of our lovely land will make a constant appeal to us to live the higher life of joy and freedom. Table Mountain, in particular, will preach this great gospel to the myriads of toilers in the valley below. And those who, whether members of the Mountain Club or not, make a habit of ascending her beautiful slopes in their free moments, will reap a rich reward not only in bodily health and strength, but also in an inner freedom and purity, in an habitual spirit of delight, which will be the crowning glory of their lives.

"May I express the hope that in the years to come this memorial will draw myriads who live down below to breathe the purer air and become better men and women. Their spirits will join with those up here, and it will make us all purer and nobler in spirit and better citizens of the country," was his verdict.

On Good Friday, 30 March 1923, he informed Margaret in his weekly letter that his "little address on Table Mountain under the title 'The Spirit of the Mountain'" a month before had made a good impression and attracted widespread attention. "The consecration of life by the spirit of joy seems somehow to be considered only a topic for poetry and not a subject for a politician with a reputation for worldliness. Some said to me that was the last thing they expected from me. And I retort by saying that when the last book is opened, I shall surprise them much more. But this is egotistical."

On 2 October 1925 Smuts was able to send Margaret a draft of his new manuscript on his concept of holism which he called "the key which unlocks the entrance to the innermost recesses of the spirit".

When his *Holism and Evolution* at last appeared in 1926, Smuts sent copies to Margaret and her husband Arthur. He explained that this first book on holism explored holism in nature and in its scientific aspects, but did not deal with its spiritual and philosophical aspects. He regarded this first book as an essential preliminary "canter over the ground", but he indicated that he might follow it up in future if he could find the time.

In the thirties Smuts did follow up his first book. He wrote four chapters of a projected work on holism of the spirit, dealing with religion and philosophy, but he did not have the time to complete it, as I will discuss in Chapter 5.

He was surprised and even taken aback when the intellectual world and even his friend Dr Kolbe branded him as irreligious because of his creation of the concept of holism in science and philosophy.

CHAPTER TWO

Smuts and the new physics

The great pity in the life of Smuts is that the new physics had not been invented when he wrote his book *Holism and Evolution*. He himself was aware of the fact that his book was to some extent based on inadequate scientific knowledge of physical reality. The reason for this was that the main thrust of scientific thinking in the West during the last three centuries had been reductionist. This meant that the scientist followed the simple expedient of breaking up life and reality to try to find its essence, while problems encountered were taken apart in an effort to solve their inherent riddles or mysteries.

Even living organisms were regarded and treated as meaningless mounds of atoms formed pointlessly and haphazardly as the result of random accidents. This led to a form of determinism which tended to put life and reality into a straightjacket which destroyed its essence, its beauty and its inner spirit and values.

Smuts rebelled against this. To him orthodox science had been too exclusively concerned with analysis, with breaking up life and reality into meaningless parts and with the synthetic reconstitution of living and non-living things from their analytical elements. In this way scientists in trying to solve the problems of life and reality destroyed the essence of their subject matter, namely the unity and wholeness of life and matter and all reality.

In his view, the process of whole-making encompasses all life and reality and also forms the basis of evolution. This makes the world and the entire universe a progressive series of wholes or individual patterns, from its physical beginnings, in the form of matter or energy, to the flowering of life in all its manifold forms and gradations.

As late as April 1938, in the preface he wrote for the German edition of *Holism and Evolution,* he admitted that when he had researched his book in the twenties, some parts of his scientific argument were not quite up to date, but he contended that in spite of that, the fundamental idea of seeing life and reality as a whole stands on a different footing.

The principle is stronger than the supporting argument and is in a sense not dependent on it. At its lowest value the argument may be looked upon as in the nature of illustrations and exemplifications rather than actual proof of the principle of holism.

"That principle is that reality is fundamentally holistic, and that all patterns of existence in which it finds expression tend to be wholes, or holistic in one degree or another."

To express and formulate this tendency of wholeness in science and philosophy Smuts, with his intimate knowledge of Greek, used the Greek word *olos* (*holos*) meaning "whole" to coin the word holism, and coupled it in his book with the evolutionary process as propounded by Charles Darwin in his book *On the Origin of Species.*

The Oxford English Dictionary in accepting holism as a new word in the English language gives full credit for inventing the word and its meaning in 1926 to J. C. Smuts. It explains the derivation of the word and says that it represents "the tendency in nature to produce wholes from the ordered grouping of units".

What is remarkable is that the modern scientists who invented and established the new physics almost sixty years after the appearance of *Holism and Evolution* also accepted the whole and wholeness as the basis and essence of life and reality, but they have not given credit to Smuts as the originator of the concept.

Foremost amongst the new physicists is Professor David Bohm of Pennsylvania whose epoch-making book *Wholeness and the Implicate Order* first appeared in 1980 in the USA and Canada and has enjoyed several reprints since then. Like Smuts 54 years earlier, Bohm is an exponent of the wholeness of the universe and against the notion of analysing the world into relatively autonomous parts. In his book he used both the relativity theory of Einstein and the postulates of the new quantum theory to stress the undivided wholeness of the universe.

The pity is that Bohm, who now lives in London where he is Professor of Theoretical Physics at Birkbeck College, for one or other reason (not stated in his book), does not use Smuts's word holism to describe this tendency towards wholeness, although like Smuts he has done research into both physics and philosophy.

Only once in his book *Wholeness and the Implicate Order* (on page 17) does Bohm use the term "holistic" to describe some fixed kind of integrating or unifying "holistic" principle of our self-world view, but he rejects its use. Instead, later on in his book he coins his own word "hologram" derived from the Greek words *holos*, meaning "whole", and *gram* meaning "to write". Thus his hologram is an instrument that, as it were, "writes the whole", as he explains it.

However, "holism" in my view is a much better and a more descriptive word than "hologram". Why can't Bohm accept it as such?

Fortunately the second contribution of the modern scientists to the wholeness of nature has fully accepted the words holism and "holistic" to describe this process. Professor Paul Davies of the University of Newcastle-upon-Tyne in his interesting book *God and the New Physics* follows Smuts's example to stress the difference between holism and reductionism in science.

He is even more outspoken than Smuts in rejecting the scientific method of taking a problem apart in order to analyse it in an attempt to solve it.

To him this is the wrong method. Some problems are only solved by putting them together – "they are synthetic or 'holistic' in nature", as he explains it.

Davies, although adopting Smuts's holism and the use of the word "holistic" to describe life, the mind and the soul of man, also does not give any credit to the brilliant and versatile South African as the father of the concept. Smuts's name is never mentioned in his book, but it is significant that he unquestioningly accepts Smuts's explanation that "the whole is greater than the sum of its parts". This is on page 6 of *God and the New Physics*.

This concept was basic to Smuts's entire theory of holism as expounded in 1926, 64 years earlier.

Although Davies gives no credit to Smuts as the originator of holism, his book *God and the New Physics* is in many respects the book Smuts wanted to write as a sequel to his first book, *Holism and Evolution*.

As I have pointed out, Smuts actually drafted four chapters of this

19

second book under the title *Holism of the Spirit*. He regarded his first book as mostly scientific in order to reveal the scientific basis of the concept of the whole in matter and reality. But in spite of the criticism that this made his *Holism and Evolution* irreligious, he knew that his concept of holism "is a sincere groping towards the spiritual core of things", as he explained in a letter to Arthur Gillett on 10 November 1926.

"Proceeding along scientific and philosophic lines I found no God of Theology at the end. But I say and recognise explicitly that the divine Ideal rests on other grounds and other evidence. Science and philosophy will not unlock the Great door but they may bring us right up to the threshold.

"Whether you can enter into the Great Mystery depends on certain attitudes, certain inner affinities, which alone can draw you in spirit into the Great Kinship of the Spirit, the inner mystic union of Holism.

"On that I say nothing in my book *Holism and Evolution*. Perhaps (if I am wise) I shall never say anything at all in writing. But I know this communion from inner experience. And I know that millions through the ages have seen and followed the unseen Inner Light.

"Some people will think that Holism is anti-theistic or godless. I don't think so, nor is that the spirit in which the book was written. That you know."

Smuts here reveals for the first time in writing his inner spiritual life, his communion with God based on inner experience. That it occurred many times in his crowded life is apparent from a close study of the massive amount of material in the form of personal letters, notes, reminiscences, speeches and sayings he left behind.

This is what he had in mind for his second book, *Holism II*, as Professor Hancock named it in his two volumes of the biography of Smuts.

There are two reasons why Smuts never completed this follow-up to *Holism and Evolution*. The first is that he was too involved with politics, wars and international events in a "most troublesome world – certainly not of my choosing", as he explained to Arthur.

The second reason, however, is more important. After the appearance of his first book Smuts realised that both Einstein's theory of relativity and the new quantum theory had opened up a new world of science with an immense extension of knowledge and insight into the essence of life and reality. What was of even greater significance was that he was aware of the important new studies, discoveries and revelations in science and religion, and more importantly in the combination of the two new theories of relativity and the quantum.

Science in the past few centuries had mainly been preoccupied with the physical world and the lower grades of the organic world. It had become mechanistic and analytical and had lost sight of the unity of life and reality as a whole, and had reduced life and the world to dead aggregations rather than to real living wholes which make up nature.

Then in 1927 Smuts, on reading Bertrand Russell's book *Analysis of Matter* which Margaret had sent to him, discovered the new quantum theory which opened a door for him. In his weekly letter to her he mentioned that Russell and he did not see eye to eye on philosophy. "He is an atomist while I am a holist. He would call holism mysticism, while I am trying from the rich resources of mysticism, to rescue this concept of holism for knowledge and science.

"But in spite of our differences, I can learn a lot from him. His attempt to connect quanta with qualities is interesting and gives me a clue for which I have long been looking. Science gives only quantities or extensive magnitudes. How do qualities or qualitative differences arise? The curious mystery of the quantum may hold the secret of this origin," was his conclusion.

As is well known, the quantum theory was discovered by the German scientist Max Planck in 1900, when he demonstrated that light waves behave in some ways like particles (photons). He used the Latin word *quanta* to describe the particles which come in indivisible lumps or packets, and formulated the quantum theory on that basis. Einstein followed in 1919 with his theory of relativity which further extended man's insight and knowledge of the mysterious universe in which we live. Einstein propounded the theory that all motion is relative. In 1925 the German scientist Erwin Schrödinger, who became Max Planck's successor in Berlin, went one step further by discovering wave mechanics, which earned him a Nobel Prize.

In the spring of 1933 when I arrived at Oxford as a Rhodes Scholar, Professor Schrödinger arrived there too and was made a fellow of Magdalen College, where he often lectured on his great discovery which had opened a new and important door to a better understanding of life and the entire universe.

21

In many respects these three great discoveries, the quantum theory, the theory of relativity and the theory of wave mechanics revolutionised the entire world of physics with important spin-offs on biology, philosophy and almost all other disciplines of learning including religion and theology.

Both Bohm in his *Wholeness and the Implicate Order* and Paul Davies in *God and the New Physics* regard the quantum and the relativity theories as the main basis of the new physics, although reference is also made to Schrödinger's wave mechanics. But both omit to give any credit to Smuts's discovery of holism, although it also forms the basis of their outlook.

Smuts as a large-hearted human being would, however, have forgiven them for this omission. In fact he would have praised them had he been alive, as both Bohm and Davies used his holistic outlook to lead science and especially the new physics into the domain of the higher ethical and spiritual values which, as I have pointed out, was Smuts's aim in his projected second book on holism of the spirit.

This is especially the case with Davies's book *God and the New Physics*. Like Smuts in his *Holism and Evolution*, Davies also points out that science and religion approach the important questions of existence from different points of view. Whereas religion is based on revelation and personal experiences and received wisdom, the scientists try to establish truth through careful observation and experiment.

It is, however, a great fallacy to deduce from this that religious people are not interested in, or are suspicious of science, or that scientists are irreligious. The true scientist like the true believer always keeps an open mind in order to discover the truth through careful observations and possible divine revelations to those who are receptive to God's love and wisdom in their lives.

This was true of Smuts. He was both a scientist and a firm believer in the mercy, the loving kindness and the power of God in his own life as in the lives of millions of peoples of all races and classes.

Smuts also expressed this belief in God and the spiritual values which religion brings into the lives of people in his great oration when the ashes of Emily Hobhouse were buried at the foot of the Vroue-monument in Bloemfontein on 26 October 1926. Pointing out how Emily Hobhouse had saved countless women and children in the

British camps during the Boer War, he reminded his listeners how often a woman appears at the decisive moment in the life of a nation and in her weakness turns the flowing tides of events.

To Smuts this is evidence of God and his mercy: "It is the inner spiritual force in the world which comes to the surface in pain and anguish and sorrow. And once it appears everything else shrinks in insignificance before it. IN THE END THE SPIRITUAL VALUES OF LIFE ARE SURPREME."

Davies admits that many professional scientists are also deeply religious and apparently have little intellectual difficulty in allowing the two sides of their philosophy peacefully to co-exist. He, however, sees a problem in translating many disparate religious experiences into a coherent religious world-view. According to him, Christian cosmology, for example, differs radically from Oriental cosmology. "At least one must be wrong," he concludes.

Here I think in all humility that Davies is mistaken. Neither the Western Christian outlook nor the Oriental outlook is wrong. Both serve their purposes of guiding their adherents towards God the Creator. Whatever He is called, there can be only one God, and many people in different parts of the world and in different centuries appeal to Him as the Father and Creator of the universe. The form in which they do so, or the dogma which they apply, may be different, but surely the spirit in which they worship God depends on their individual experiences, wishes and desires.

It must also be remembered that Jesus revealed that God is a Spirit and they who worship Him must worship Him in spirit and truth. This He explained to the woman of Samaria who came to draw water at Jacob's well, as described in John 4:24.

Many years ago Aldous Huxley published a book with the title *The Perennial Philosophy*. It is an anthology of writings from mystics from various periods and various religions in different parts of the world. One can open it anywhere and find beautiful utterances of a similar kind. What is remarkable is the almost miraculous agreement between humans of different races, different religions, different outlooks. They are separated from one another by place and time, living in different parts of the globe or in different centuries, but in their worship of God there is the same spirit of humility, of adoration, of love, mercy and faith. Of course the formalities and the dogma of the

23

various religions are different, but religion is not form and dogma, it is in its inner essence faith, worship and adoration.

This was also Smuts's view. He was deeply religious, with an inner conviction and one can say a personal contact with God through thought and prayer, but with little formality or dogma.

Smuts, brought up on a Boland farm in the Cape Province, was christened in and became a member of the Dutch Reformed Church, married in the Church and had his nine children also christened in the Church. When he was a student at Cambridge he regularly attended the Presbyterian Church. I recently received a letter from his old friend Jan B. Gillett – named Jan, after Smuts – reminding me of this fact. He added that a woman friend from northern England was with Smuts at Cambridge. Smuts evidently wrote a letter to her about his attendance at the Presbyterian Church, but she forgot to forward his letter to the Smuts collection. Both as a student at Stellenbosch and later at Cambridge he studied Greek.

This led to a clearer grasp and understanding of the insight and revelations of Jesus as the basis of the Christian religion. It gave him a lifelong faith in God with a deep admiration for the genius of Jesus as the personification of God and the highest personality which life has brought forth. He was especially glad in his middle life through his friendship with Emily Hobhouse to make contact with the Quakers of Street in Somersetshire in England where he observed their lack of dogma and formalities and admired their method of silent worship, prayer and meditation. This corresponded with his basic outlook in regarding religion as an inner experience where through communion in silence and silent prayer contact is established with God the Father and also with the power of the Holy Spirit in the lives of people as revealed by Jesus Christ.

In my contact and friendship with members of the Quakers I had personal experience of this quality of the presence of God through Christ in the lives of people. On one occasion after the death of Smuts in 1950 I visited Mrs Margaret Clark Gillett and her son Jan. At the time I was doing research into the life of Smuts and especially into his religious views. I was aware of their weekly letter-writing from 1919 almost to the time of his death.

We were sitting on the green lawn under a mulberry tree in her garden in Street and she told me of their great friendship which began in

24

1906 and how in almost all the letters between them religion and especially the example, the personality and the power and revelations of Jesus formed the main topic. Inevitably the power of the Holy Spirit in the lives of people was mentioned. And then suddenly she said to me: "I feel that the Holy Spirit is with us here and now."

This struck me as a moment of truth. It was almost as if I could feel the Holy Spirit upon us and as if Smuts was also there with us.

During his long life Smuts was always interested in the power of the Holy Spirit upon people, and in the domain of science he thought that telepathy as well as thought transference should be investigated and studied. In April 1925 he received from Mrs Eleanor Sidgwick, wife of the principal of Newnham College, a report on thought transference experiments. He thought that this report pointed to the limitations of our present science compared to the facts they are intended to explain. "To my mind telepathy is a great new fact which calls for readjustment of old views and new categories of explanation," he stated in a letter to her.

He himself seemed to have had some personal experiences of thought transference and telepathy. In the English summer of 1924 Margaret and her husband enjoyed a holiday at Porthcothan on the north coast of Cornwall near Newquay. They were staying in an ancient meeting house of the Society of Friends (the new name for the Quakers) at Falmouth. The house bore the name Come to Good. They enjoyed a lovely holiday and both wrote friendly letters to Smuts.

On 17 September 1924 he replied to their letters and wrote them: "Porthcothan seems to have stimulated you both very strangely, and I have felt the glow of your beings as far as 7 000 miles away. How I would have loved to have gone with you on Sundays over that strange dreamy or sleeping country to meetings in the distant villages. And what a splendid name is 'Come to Good'!

"We have so many places that might appropriately be called after the legend: Go to the Devil, but Come to Good sounds so comforting that even the sound makes you feel inclined to be happy."

A week later on 25 September 1924 he informed Margaret that their final letter from Porthcothan had arrived. "You have become almost lyrical about the place and its surroundings." He would like to sample it himself on some future occasion, not omitting a visit to Come to Good.

He himself had spent two delightful weeks at home on his farm Doornkloof at Irene. "Nothing but reading and riding and a little writing all the day. The reading is mostly botanical and biological, though physical speculations have not escaped me."

He then told Margaret that he had read all the books she had sent him in recent years, including Einstein "whom I begin to understand thoroughly. I only believe it ought to be possible to devise some simpler scheme to explain the unitary character of time, space, matter and all physical appearances and activities. I have never yet applied holism in this domain, which is so purely mathematical."

Smuts at this time was also president of the South African Association for the Advancement of Science, which was founded in 1903 in Cape Town. In this position he was deeply interested in the important discovery of the Taung fossil which was regarded as an anthropological breakthrough. He congratulated Professor Dart in a letter of 4 February 1925 on this discovery, which in his opinion was likely to concentrate attention on South Africa as a great field for scientific discovery, following on the unique importance for human evolution of the Rhodesian Broken Hill skull discovered a little earlier. "It seems to open up a still further vista into our human past," was his verdict.

Then on 23 September 1931 at the centenary meeting of the British Association for the Advancement of Science Smuts delivered the presidential address entitled "The Scientific World Picture of Today".

As president of this association he was also asked to preside at the Faraday Centenary Exhibition at the Royal Albert Hall in London to celebrate the discovery of the production of electricity from magnetism on 28 August 1831, as well as at the Clerk Maxwell Centenary to commemorate the birth in 1831 of James Clerk Maxwell, the Scottish physicist, best known for his theory of electromagnetic waves.

It was indeed a great honour for the South African leader to preside at these three important scientific centenaries and to give the presidential address to the assembled scientists of England. Here Smuts was recognised and honoured not as a politician or a statesman, but as a scientist himself with his remarkable discovery of holism as a key to the understanding of science and life.

What is even more important is that he rose to the great occasion with one of the most brilliant orations of his career. Even now his address can be read and appreciated as a thought-provoking insight into and explanation of the riddles and mysteries of science as of life. He himself regarded the celebration as a milestone which enabled scientists to look back on a hundred years of scientific progress such as has no parallel in history.

"It brings us to a point in the advance from which we can confidently look forward to fundamental solutions and discoveries in the near future, which may transform the entire field of science," was his confident prediction which in many ways has been fulfilled.

With his remarkable sense of history Smuts pointed out that nineteenth-century science was in fact a system of purified, glorified common sense. But underneath the placid surface, the scientific seeds of the future were germinating and with the coming of the twentieth century fundamental changes began to set in. "The new point of departure was reached when physical science ceased to confine its attention to the things that are observed. It dug down to a deeper level, and below the things that appear to the senses, it found, or invented, at the base of the world, so-called scientific entities, not capable of direct observation, but which are necessary to account for the facts of observations."

He pointed out that below molecules and atoms still more ultimate entities appeared, such as radiations, electrons and protons, which form and underlie our world of matter. Matter itself practically disappeared into energy; all the material forms of sky and earth and sea were dissolved and spirited away into the "blue of energy". Two of his predecessors in the chair, Sir Joseph John Thomson and Lord Rutherford, were outstanding among the scientists who brought about this important transformation.

In this connection both Faraday and Clerk Maxwell, with the celebrated equations of the electromagnetic field which applied to light no less than to electromagnetism, led the way to Minkowski's amazing discovery in 1908 that time and space were not separate things, but constitute elements in the deeper synthesis of space-time. This brought about a great change in the perception of the world.

After this explanation, Smuts concentrated his review on the brilliant discoveries of Albert Einstein with his relativity theory and Max Planck with his quantum theory. He pointed out that the concept of space-time in the hands of Einstein led beyond Euclid and Newton to the recasting of the law and the concept of gravitation and to the new relativity conception of the basic structure of the world.

27

This transformation of the concept of space, owing to the injection into it of time, had destroyed the old passive homogeneous notion of space and had substituted a flexible variable continuum, the curvatures and unevennesses of which constitute to our senses what we call a material world. The new concept had made it possible to construe matter, mass and energy as but definite measurable conditions of curvature in the structure of space-time. There could be no doubt about the immense possibilities it had opened up, he predicted.

He then moved on to the even more revolutionary advance in physics made possible by Max Planck's discovery of the quantum theory, according to which energy is granular, consisting of discrete grains or *quanta*. The world in space-time is a continuum; the quantum action is a negation of continuity. The quantum appears to behave like a particle, but a particle out of space or time. As Sir Arthur Eddington graphically puts it: a quantum of light is large enough to fill the lens of a hundred-inch telescope, but it is also small enough to enter an atom. It may spread like a circular wave through the universe, but when it hits its mark, the cosmic wave instantaneously contracts to a point where it strikes with its full and undivided force.

Smuts summarised his remarks by saying that the vastly improved technique of research had led to physical discoveries which had at last completely shattered the traditional common sense view of our material world which had held sway in the nineteenth century. A new space-time world had emerged which was essentially immaterial, and in which the old-time matter, and even the scientific mass, gravitation and energy stood for no independent entities but could best be construed as configurations of space-time, while the discovery of the quantic properties of the world pointed to still more radical transformations which loomed on the horizon of science. The complete recasting of many of our categories of experience and thought might ultimately be involved.

He further pointed out that there had also been advances in the biological sciences with the discovery of organic evolution. Space-time finds its natural completion in organic evolution, and thus the world, due to the new scientific outlook, becomes a process, where nothing ever remains the same or is a duplicate of anything else, but appears as a growing, gathering, creative stream of unique events which rolls forever forward.

He went on to link this new outlook in science to the world of the human spirit with its great values and ideals. "Besides science we have other forms of the inner relation between the mind and the universe, such as poetry, music, art and religion. The human spirit is not a pathetic wandering phantom of the universe, but is at home, and meets with spiritual hospitality and responses everywhere. Our deepest thoughts and emotions and endeavours are but responses to stimuli which come to us not from an alien, but from an essentially friendly and kindred universe," he informed his scientific listeners.

Smuts gave this oration in 1931, five years after the publication of *Holism and Evolution* which he had first drafted during his student days in the latter half of the nineteenth century, when the scientific world picture was entirely different and almost entirely based on determinism and materialism.

This was one reason why he was anxious to write a sequel: to incorporate the important new discoveries. He realised that the iron determination of the older science, so contrary to direct human experience, so destructive of the free activity of life and mind, as well as subversive to the moral responsibility of the individual, had been materially recast. Relativity reduces substance to configuration or patterns, while quantum physics gives definite indications of indeterminism in nature.

Meanwhile, life through all the ages clearly shows a creative advance to ever more complex organisations, and ever higher qualities, while mind is responsible for the creation of a whole realm of values. "We are thus justified in stressing, along with natural necessity, an increasing measure of freedom and creativeness in the world, sufficient to account for organic evolution and for the appearance of moral law and endeavour. This liberation of life and the spirit from the iron rule of necessity is one of the greatest gains from the recent scientific advances."

It was on this new scientific basis that Smuts was anxious to write his sequel to *Holism and Evolution* to explain the relation between life and mind and the physical universe and to link man through his spiritual background with the Spirit of God as the creator of the universe and the giver of life.

Instead of an animistic, mechanistic or mathematical universe, the new science had created, in his view, a genetic, organic, holistic universe. In this holistic scheme man is in every truth the offspring of the stars. "The world consists not only of electrons and radiations, but also of souls and aspirations. Beauty and holiness are as much aspects of nature as energy and entropy. Thus 'in eternal lines to time it [the world] grows'." Such, in vague outline, was the world-picture to which science seemed to be pointing, he concluded.

CHAPTER THREE

Smuts's personal religion

There are two aspects of religion in the life of Smuts, namely his personal religion and his deep interest in the philosophy of religion. In my book *The Holistic Smuts*, I dealt mostly with the latter, as there are numerous references in his writings and speeches to religion as a subject of interest, study and contemplation from the point of view of philosophy.

In my personal contact with him during the last twelve years of his life, I found him reluctant to discuss personal matters. He was naturally averse to and even suspicious of personal enquiries into his life and especially his religion. Even in his letters to his wife, Isie, he seldom mentioned his religion or religious subjects.

But what is remarkable is that he had no reluctance to discuss both his personal religion and his philosophic interest in religious matters in his letters to his "best friend" Margaret Clark and her sister Alice. In most of his weekly letters to Margaret over a period of 31 years from 1919 to his death in 1950 he indulged in religious discussions and personal confessions of the hand of God in his life. These letters thus provide a unique record of his personal faith in God.

Professor Hancock, in referring to Smuts's references to religion in his letters to Margaret and other friends, claimed that he was not writing philosophical or theological dissertations, but was flinging into his letters almost at random ideas which welled up within him as he read his Greek New Testament.

What is also remarkable is that this mostly happened when Smuts was in a crisis in time of war or other calamities. As Hancock puts it: "Always his concentration was most intense in times of crisis. Whenever the visible became clouded over, he vividly apprehended the invisible."

31

In the aftermath of the disaster of Tobruk in the Second World War when the German General Erwin Rommel defeated the South African forces in North Africa, Smuts found personal strength in the Epistle which Paul wrote to the Hebrews. In Chapter 11, verse 22, Paul speaks of seeing the Invisible.

To Smuts this was the result of Paul's faith in God. "Faith", he wrote to Margaret, "becomes so strong that it is no longer faith, no longer a longing and groping but a seeing of something real and present and waiting to be disclosed."

Here Smuts revealed the inner core, the driving spirit of his faith in God. As I mentioned in *The Holistic Smuts*, he was deeply influenced by the writings of Paul during the Second World War when he felt the need to strengthen his faith against Hitlerism, but it started much earlier in his life.

In the next chapter which deals with the personality of Jesus, I will discuss Smuts's lifelong interest in and contemplation of the genius of Jesus. I will show the influence and the power of Jesus in his life and in his holism. But now I wish to do justice to his personal religion, his belief in God, his trust in the Almighty, his use of prayer and his occasional revelations of the power of the Holy Spirit in his life.

The readers of *The Holistic Smuts*, especially the chapter on Smuts as the holistic man, will know what a deeply religious person he really was. But like Paul, Smuts had to be spiritually reborn before he found his soul and before he was ready for his life's task.

The conflicts and tragedies of the Boer War and its ruinous aftermath touched him deeply. What suffering he must have endured, what depths he must have sounded before he reached the new life of the reborn. "I learnt to bow my head to the inevitable," was how he explained the transformation which came over him. Like Job in the Bible, Smuts after years of brooding and despair learnt to accept the will of God, he bowed to the inevitable and God in his time rewarded him with greater gifts of friendship, understanding and wisdom.

He himself in a revealing passage in his book *Holism and Evolution* described the tremendous effect on the "moral awakening" in the life of a person when he first hears the trumpet call of duty. It is then that the still small voice of the inner life comes to the fore and a person learns to be himself with perfect honesty, integrity and sincerity and "earnest men find that to gain their life they must lose it, that not in self, but in

32

the whole (including the self) lies the only upward road to the sunlit summits."

Smuts here crossed his Rubicon, he became a "universal man", as Shakespeare, Goethe and Leonardo da Vinci were universal men and as Dr Albert Schweitzer was a universal man of our time. This happened in 1906 when he was 36 years old, and was mostly as a result of his personal contacts with the Quakers in England.

Although Smuts never became a Quaker and remained a member of the Dutch Reformed Church, he was spiritually deeply influenced by the Quaker outlook, but also differed from them on the use of force.

In his first letter to Margaret on 6 September 1919 from Cape Town after his return to South Africa he referred to his religion: "Life to me has been very great and sweet and true. And I thank God for all I have gone through – the great fires of life which purge the soul and feed it with the food immortal."

Shortly after his return he had his first revelation. On 4 October 1919 he wrote to Margaret: "The day before yesterday when I was coming through my own native parts, now in full flower, a flood of emotions surged over my soul, and I had again that great experience in which Downs mixed with Veld and I felt uplifted beyond the limits of time and space." ("Downs" refers to the Quaker country in the South of England and "Veld" to his favourite fields in South Africa.)

When he addressed the South African Zionist Federation on 3 November 1919 in Johannesburg he praised the Jewish people for their faith in God. His main theme was that "all great things in the world are done in faith".

On 10 January 1920 he wrote to Margaret's sister Alice that his mind and his heart were simply torn with pity over all the measureless human misery in the world. "I believe in God and I believe in Jesus. But dear Alice, I am often very low and despondent over it all . . . where God rings down the curtain and darkness settles once more on human destiny."

On 6 December 1921 in a letter to Margaret and her husband, Arthur, Smuts again stressed the importance of faith in difficult times: "Let us have faith. 'The Lord advances and ever advances,' as Walt Whitman says. Why should we assume that just now He is in retreat?"

And then in 1922 Smuts's faith in God and his spiritual friendship

33

with the Quakers were severely tested when he felt compelled to resort to force and bloodshed to quell the miners' strike on the Rand.

I have already referred to this unfortunate development. He defended his action in letters to both Margaret and Alice. Margaret forgave him but Alice as a strict Quaker could not accept the use of force and stopped writing her cheerful letters to Smuts. However, he and Margaret continued their weekly letters.

In his letter to Margaret on 30 August 1922 he begged "God to have mercy on this poor soiled world".

On Good Friday (30 March 1923) he informed Margaret that he intended spending the day on Table Mountain. "It is one of those wonderful days that sends a subdued thrill through you from the time you get out of bed. You feel like singing, and even the humble task of shaving seems somehow to share in the delight. It will be great on the mountain."

On 11 May 1925 he wrote to Margaret about a visit to Caledon, a small town in the Cape, where he had been scheduled to open a political party bazaar. Here again his deep religious nature came to the fore both in his acceptance of God in his life and the effect nature and especially mountains had on his inner happiness. It is a beautiful testimony of adoration as can be seen from passages in the letter. He and his political friend, Deneys Reitz, who later became famous as the author of the two books, *On Commando* and *Trekking On*, had motored from Cape Town to attend and open the political rally after a very arduous week in Parliament in Cape Town.

"We were both sick about this new labour . . . but the day was gorgeous, such a May day as you get in this land of God. And we gradually cheered up as we motored along," he wrote to Margaret.

He opened the bazaar, they lunched and Neysie (as Deneys was called) made "a good speech. And then after lunch I looked at that great mountain behind Caledon (known as the Klein Swartberg) and my heart took flight, I said to the good people I was going up the mountain. They stared at me in astonishment. 'It was too rough, I would lose my way. Nobody went up there.'

"So I went up by myself, accompanied by my thoughts and memories, with the flowers and rare ericas and proteas smiling at me. Up and up until I was on the top and viewed the glorious landscape in that perfect air, and heard the grysbok [a small grey antelope] whistle

34

and 'was made one with nature' as Shelley described the feeling in his poem 'Adonis'.

"Then I came down a little way, took off my clothes, which are alien to that sort of surrounding and had a glorious sunbathe. I gathered many plants, and laden with inner and outward treasures I arrived back at Caledon in the evening. And then dinner and once more speeches till midnight.

"But I was satisfied because I had been refreshed by contact with the Great Happiness. On Sunday morning we motored back to Cape Town in perfect weather once more, and in the afternoon you would have found me once more grappling with the problems of holism."

As a footnote he mentioned that there were over a hundred varieties of ericas, wild flowers indigenous to South Africa, and at Caledon the yellow *Erica jasminiflora* is a rare local variety much sought after by botanists. He must have collected some specimens on the mountain.

Apart from his interest in wild flowers, mountaineering, religion and his parliamentary duties as the leader of the opposition, Smuts was also rewriting his manuscript on holism which was published a year later, while he also found time to write a treatise on science from the South African point of view which was published in the November issue of the *South African Journal of Science*.

To his friend and former private secretary Ernest Lane he explained in a letter on 1 July 1925 that his concept of holism was largely original and might prove of some scientific and philosophical value. He sent several copies of his manuscript to Lane asking him to look for a publisher in England. He also sent a copy to Margaret, explaining to her that the holism which interested her – its spiritual and philosophical aspects – was not yet in his first manuscript.

As already mentioned, in the thirties – after the appearance of *Holism and Evolution* and its favourable reception by the scientific community – Smuts wrote four chapters of a projected book on the spiritual and philosophical aspects of holism, but he never completed the book. It was at this time too that in the afterglow of the appearance of *Holism and Evolution*, Smuts revealed his deep interest in the Christian religion. In a letter of 10 November 1926 to his friend Arthur Gillett he revealed his communion from inner experience.

It is a remarkable letter in many ways as a revelation of the working of his mind. His holism had previously been attacked by his close friend Dr F. C. Kolbe, who had left the Dutch Reformed ministry to become a Roman Catholic.

When Kolbe first read *Holism and Evolution* he was very impressed by it and he said to a friend "This is a deeply religious book." He wrote this in a letter to Smuts on 31 December 1926. Later Kolbe changed his mind and objected to passages in the book, one of which was Smuts's statement that the creative process is necessarily always upward and forward. Kolbe thought it might also degenerate and become stagnant in the case of the earth, as had happened to the moon and other planets.

His main objection was, however, that Smuts accepted Kant's "blunder", as he called it, that from the facts of nature no inference to a transcendent mind – in other words a God – is justified. Smuts was, however, convinced that holism was a sincere groping towards the spiritual core of things.

It was shortly after this that Margaret sent him a copy of Bertrand Russell's book *Analysis of Matter* which was published in 1927. Smuts read it eagerly and on 31 August 1927 he informed Margaret that he found the book very well worth careful study.

In the summer of 1932 Margaret had visited Land's End in Cornwall and attended the ancient festival known as Flurry, named after a wonderful dance called Helston Flurry which probably originated as a ceremony to purge the houses of evil. He was very impressed by her letter which unfortunately is not available. It is probable that she asked him if he believed in prayer for, in his reply on 4 June 1932, he suddenly wrote:

"Yes, I believe in prayer – not in the variety which tries to cajole or circumvent the deity, but in the unutterable longing and waiting for the reality behind it all and in reunion with that whole to which we belong. We are but temporary moments in the eternal current of being, and in the thought of that whole there is rest and blessedness and refreshment for us. Surely prayer is this mystic reunion and escape from the bonds of our mere individual being into Being itself."

He then went on to ask Margaret to get him a copy of *What I Owe to Christ*, the new book by C. F. Andrews, the friend of Mahatma Gandhi. The reviewer of the book in *The Manchester Guardian* said that no such book had been written for a long time. Smuts wrote: "I am always deeply interested in that sort of thing. The last and highest

36

phase of holism is religion and the subject is often in my mind. But it is a conception of religion which is very unorthodox – almost a religion without God, I fear.

"The ordinary terms of religion are so vibrated by popular use that one likes to avoid them and state our pure human experience in fresh terminology. But at bottom I do firmly believe that all the great spirits of the world have felt the same thing and passed through the same phases of inner life. I think holism is a great clue in these matters if one only had the time and the ability to work it out fully. In the end the religious motif remains the deepest in human life.

"At present it appears to be all economics; finance dominates the world. And yet I feel that in the end we shall have to evolve a deeper and truer religious outlook if man has to save his soul. We live by faith, we feed on ideals, and nothing else in the end will satisfy us. I think the New Testament can be modernised in holistic language and thus rid it of all antiquarianism which now sounds so strange and far off to us, trained as we are in a modern outlook. Of course it will take generations of groping, of trial and error before we once more see a clear light. But I have no doubt that it will come and that it is the one thing necessary."

He went on to reject communism, saying that the faith in which he was brought up remained the only creed for him – human liberty, personal initiative and the spirit of adventure, and not safety first. What was wanted in the world was a new spirit of service, of human service. " 'The soul is for ever', as Walt Whitman, the American poet, said. Nothing can take its place. This may sound old-fashioned, but it has been the faith and the vision of our best for thousands of years."

Another female friend of Smuts to whom he wrote about religion was Mrs Florence Lamont of the USA. Her husband, Tom Lamont, was a banker who travelled a great deal and she often met Smuts when he travelled overseas. When not together they often wrote letters on religion. On 29 April 1934 he informed Florence that as rector of St Andrews University he had to be in Scotland the following September and October to deliver his rectorial address. If she and Tom would be in England at that time it might be possible for them to see more of each other. "There is so much to talk about, so many notes to compare, and life is so short, and so little of it remains in any case. Ah me, what gnats we are to buzz around problems we never solve. And we neglect the great perennial problems of the personal life which at bottom are the most important of all. Economics pass by; the human soul remains for ever, the centre of our human universe. Is it not the very essence of the Christian message that the soul is the great thing?" He then quoted from Mark 8:36: "For what shall it profit a man, if he shall gain the whole world, and lose his own soul?"

To this he added "But of course by souls we no longer mean personal salvation, but rather the great spiritual ideals which have been the very life-blood of our civilization, and there our failure today is even more poignant than our economic chaos."

In a letter of 9 July 1934 to Margaret he repeated his belief that faith in "something Good beyond is the greatest thing in the world. There is some harmony at the heart of the universe . . . and the vision of God is the lure of the universe, the Eros of which Plato and Whitehead speak. As Job wrote in Job, chapter 13 verse 15 'Though He slay me, yet will I trust in Him'. Have ever deeper words been wrung out of the human soul by sorrow and anguish? Through sorrow and suffering and defeat mankind is finding its soul."

It was at this time that the well-known writer Sarah Gertrude Millin began writing a biography of Smuts in two volumes. She had previously completed a volume on Cecil John Rhodes. Writing to Margaret on 28 April 1935, Smuts was worried about her presentation of himself, "knowing so little of me as she really does. The only people who could tell the truth about me and know me are Isie and you. And you are dumb oracles."

Later in this letter he warned Margaret that Sarah was anxious to see her to discuss him. He, however, had not encouraged Sarah to trouble Margaret. "The story of the inner life is of course hidden from her, and I don't know if she is really interested in it," was his summing up of Sarah's efforts to present him. This may explain why when her two volumes on Smuts appeared there was little or nothing about his religion, or his inner life.

In May of 1935 Dr F. C. Kolbe sent him three articles which he had written for the *Southern Cross* newspaper on "Our Treasury of Prayer". Smuts was very pleased with this gesture of goodwill from his friend who had criticised his book *Holism and Evolution*.

On 16 July 1935 he replied to Kolbe: "Your letter was more than welcome and 'Our Treasury of Prayer' was read and reread several times. I agree with you as to the significance of prayer. In many ways it is the most intimate and unique expression of our personality. Things we dare not say to our friends, not even to ourselves, we pour out in prayer to the Mother Soul of our soul. And although I am not acquainted with the Catholic prayers, I am deeply versed in the Psalms of the Old Testament, which seem to me the greatest and noblest outpourings of the human spirit ever put into language. The inexpressible finds expression there. The soul is greatest when it returns to rest and solace in its primal source, and even language then transcends its ordinary range of expression. Of course it is all truly holistic. When the broken fragment returns to its niche in the whole it reaches a new consummation."

On 29 June 1936 he followed up this reference to holism and prayer in a letter to Margaret. He told her that he had received a letter from a Dutch professor telling him that holism was making rapid strides in Europe and was becoming more and more accepted as the position in sciences. He added that now in 1936 he had a clearer vision of what holism meant than he had had twelve years previously when he wrote *Holism and Evolution*, just as his effort of 1925 was an advance on that of 1910 when he first discovered the idea of the whole and originated the concept of holism.

"The philosophical implications of the idea have given me a good deal of trouble during the last few years. I believe the key to religion is to be found along holistic lines, but the subject is full of pitfalls, and one hesitates to write about it."

During the Second World War, when he was under enormous pressure he redefined the importance of prayer. In a letter to Margaret on 29 November 1942 he wrote: "For the old slogan 'watch and pray' I shall have to substitute 'watch and work' which is a much more arduous business. Prayer is often resorted to as a form of escape from hard endeavour. In that sense it is a source of weakness and not strength and refreshment and illumination as prayer normally should be. Prayer is a very holistic function, and more than many other forms of activity establishes our contact with the whole – it is a nexus of part of the whole, and a spiritual nexus of the deepest significance. I think the old religious slogan was *laborare est orare* (to work is to pray) and that expresses more accurately what I consider should be our attitude."

It is significant that Smuts in the years before, during and after the Second World War made few references to his personal religion. What is equally remarkable was that his main concentration and emphasis during these tempestuous times shifted to an intense interest in, study and exploration of the miracle, the power and the guidance of the divine personality of Jesus, in the lives of people and in his own life. In the next chapter I shall deal with this vital aspect of his personal religion.

CHAPTER FOUR

The influence of the power and personality of Jesus on Smuts's life

Throughout his life of 80 years Jan Smuts was interested in an enquiry into and a study of personality. This also formed the essence of his concept of holism where the evolvement of the human personality in its wholeness as a free and harmonious self-realisation became the *summum bonum* of holism.

In his preface to the German edition of *Holism and Evolution* written in 1938 he stated the conviction "borne in upon me by a life time of thought and active participation in affairs that the way of reform, the way of salvation lies through the fostering, the purification, the enrichment of the human personality. There the Divine Light shines most clearly in the dark world."

And to him as a devoted Christian, Jesus was the highest, the purest, the noblest and the most divine personality who had walked our earth and revealed to mankind the way to and the love of God the Father and the Creator of the universe.

Especially in times of crisis, when the fate of nations and mankind in general was hanging in the balance and he as a leader became involved and was forced to take momentous decisions, the spiritual power and the divine personality of Jesus rose before him as a beacon of light and wisdom to guide his thoughts and his decisions and actions.

This is most clearly shown in his intimate letters to his friends and especially to Margaret Clarke Gillett to whom he revealed his inner life in practically every letter he wrote to her. It is in these letters that the power and the personality of Jesus form the main evidence for his deep interest in religion.

In *The Holistic Smuts*: *A Study in Personality*, I devoted a great deal of space to religion, as he was always interested in the subject from a philosophical point of view. This was because he regarded religion and spiritual values as vital for the development of personality.

To stress this point of view he coined the new word "personology", a hybrid from the Latin word *persona*, denoting the legal status of an individual who, according to Roman Law, is clothed with rights and duties in his own right, and the Greek word *logos* (meaning "word") which denotes knowledge or science. By combining the two words and concepts from the Roman and Greek civilisations he thought that he had the explanation for the ideal person in the holistic sense.

But it is remarkable that Smuts never applied his new concept of personology to Jesus. In a letter to Margaret on 3 April 1937 he expressed his deep admiration for Jesus as follows:

"Whatever one's line of interpretation and whatever one's view point, the story of Jesus remains the most mysterious and amazing of all in the human record. I don't believe there is any other which even distantly approaches it. An appropriate interpretation for our age might render a first-class service. For in the message of Jesus lies embedded what is most precious in our human insights."

It was at this time that he was again reading the New Testament in the original Greek. He did this to see whether he could obtain some fresh insights into the Gospel story, which he regarded as one of the most interesting and intriguing, but also mysterious, human documents in the long history of mankind.

"With unorthodox eyes, but with a broader view of what is essential in our human situation in all its complexity I should like to go once more through that Galilean vision of God and man. As a romance, as a Utopia, it would be the most wonderful in the world. But the remarkable thing is that it is not meant as either, but as a sober unvarnished account of the plain practical truth."

Six months later, on 8 October 1937, he returned to a discussion of the miracle of Jesus with Margaret. She had meanwhile also reread the New Testament and wrote to him from Madeira that she was shocked by some sections in Matthew's account. Smuts's reaction was that this did not surprise him. Jesus was very human and Jesus was a Jew. He should not be judged on this basis, "but by his insight and grandeur, his vision of a new God-filled world, his determination to fulfil his mission at whatever cost. He still remains the highlight of the human race.

"Comparing him to the good and the great I have known in my experience the wonder of him continues to grow on me. 'The kingdom of God is within you' – was ever a greater revelation vouchsafed to this poor erring race of man? If we could today recapture that vision how different this sad world would be. I do believe in Jesus and in a humble way I love him though not in the manner of my childhood sixty years ago.

"The mystery of the world has since come home to me, and what was simple and plain then is today very profound and mysterious."

All these letters I have quoted from so far were written in the years before the outbreak of the Second World War in 1939 and before he was again prime minister of South Africa. But when the war started in 1939 he became not only prime minister, but also the commander in chief of the South African military forces. As such his responsibilities increased enormously, while his counsel and advice were also constantly sought by the Allied countries and especially by his close friend Winston Churchill.

The result was that he came under immense pressure and in the many dramas and ups and downs of the war situation he found solace and comfort in his religion and in his constant contemplation of the life and personality of Jesus and the legacy he left behind for the salvation of mankind. In most of his weekly letters he informed Margaret of this and explained his inner life and thoughts in detail.

In his letter of 24 January 1940 he replied to Margaret's query as to what a future settlement of the war would entail. She had mentioned a federation as a possibility. To this he replied: "Can there be an institutional change where there is no change of the spirit? Can we build effectively except from the depths of the human spirit? Is Jesus not right, and is it not at bottom a spiritual issue, just as it is a spiritual disease from which we are suffering? And yet some constitutional form or mechanism must accompany the inner change of spirit."

Later he continued: "I am so afraid of false visions. My recent studies of the times of Jesus have shown me how dangerous it is to cherish vain hopes and illusions as an escape from great disasters and sufferings. The Messianic idea which emerged from the Dispersion and the Maccabean success proved the undoing of Israel in the end.

"They were always looking for the Messiah, missed the real one, and followed false ones until they were finally crushed and finished.

It is a curious story, in which Jesus forms a link and was by his own people mistaken for one of the false ones. Some false Messianic hope may emerge from the present world despair," he warned.

On 7 April 1940 he again explained Jesus' point of view on the problems of life: "I am always somewhat puzzled by the weird idea of being 'saved'. The Jews wanted to be saved from punishment for breaches of the Law, and the pagans wanted personal salvation from the evils incident to morbid ideas and practices. But surely all this belongs to an outlook that is dead and gone. What appeared to them impossible in this world was looked for and hoped for in the next.

"Jesus himself appears to have had another point of view – the new order and the new society in the Kingdom of God on this earth. It was a thoroughly social idea, and immortality was linked up with the new immortal order of God which was to come soon, very soon perhaps before that generation had passed.

"It was something like Shelley's vision of the new earth in 'Prometheus Unbound', only more deeply spiritual. If the Gospel story as we have it is to be taken at its face value Jesus had a spiritual vision of this reign of God on earth, and his sacrifice might be the event to precipitate events and bring about this change. It is only his words on the Cross ('Why hast Thou forsaken me') that makes me suspect that He hoped or expected the sacrifice would not be actually completed and that God would appear before the crisis. It is difficult to say; but in any case it is more the coming of the Kingdom than the question of immortality that interested Him in his Great Vision."

In a letter of 14 April 1941 Smuts informed Margaret that he had brought with him to Groote Schuur, his official residence in Cape Town, a copy of Renan's well-known book *Life of Jesus* which was first published in 1863. It was the second time he had read it and he found it more interesting than when he had read it a lifetime before.

"Renan is a wonderful master of language, and carries you over the rough places in the narrative with immense power."

However, he found Renan especially severe on Jesus for his crude economic views, his exaltation of the poor and the illiterate, his depreciation of property and his lack of understanding of the vast apparatus of an advanced civilisation.

"Of course this is all very true, but Jesus shows the power of the neglected factors, the importance of the unknown or forgotten man, and the strength there is in the economically lower levels of human society."

This reminded Smuts of the German poet Goethe when he pointed out in his book *Wilhelm Meister* that the pagan civilisations worshipped what was above us (the gods); the philosophers emphasised what was on a level with us, and Christianity what was below us – the common man, the common human virtues, the pain and sorrow which train the soul for higher things.

Smuts told Margaret that he had the feeling that the deepest aspects of the inner life escaped Renan, and that his insight was not equal to his literary and other gifts. And beyond everything else one comes to that deepest insight which Jesus unfolded to man – that "God so loved the world". "It is such an overwhelming insight that the power of this universe is no other than love, and that it is directed not to the glories, but to the humble creatures of God . . ."

In his letter of 23 September 1941 Smuts attacked those writers like Arnold Toynbee and others who advocated social and economic reforms to improve the conditions of life and regarded human nature as too permanent a factor to change. "I agree with their conclusions but not with the premise that human nature is so fixed and unchangeable as all that.

"Nothing is more flexible and capable of change than human nature. All Christianity, all reform is ultimately based on that flexibility. 'Repent ye,' as John the Baptist said, as Jesus said after him, change of mind, change of heart in the individual is the basis of all real advance, and it was on this fulcrum that Jesus founded his Kingdom.

"I notice a strong tendency nowadays to ignore this basic truth – that the individual soul or personality is the point of departure in human regeneration – and that the reform of society and institutions is in comparison secondary. The pendulum has swung too far. We must begin with ourselves if we wish to start on the journey of reform."

Sometime in January 1942 Smuts also again read Seeley's well-known book *Ecce Homo* which was first published in 1886. He had previously read it when he was a student at Cambridge, and now 50 years later he enjoyed it even more. He compared it to Renan's *Life of Jesus* and came to the conclusion that Seeley had a much deeper insight into the real meaning of that great movement started by Jesus, in spite of Renan's much greater scholarship and knowledge of biblical times.

"Seeley describes the drive behind the new religion as the 'enthusiasm of humanity or the passion for humanity which characterised Jesus'. Jesus had not only the insight of a great genius into spiritual values, but the spiritual energy which springs from passionate devotion, and which He could communicate to his followers and which burnt like a flame in their hearts too.

"I describe it as the Vision of God, and the desire for God which He translated into terms of love. The New Testament is really the new vision of God and the New Testament of Love. It is curious how real the gospels become to us now, with all the wracking experience of this generation.

"Once more we are sounding the depths and reaching to the real foundations below the veneer of our modern outlook and culture. The social gospel of Jesus still remains the standard and ideal for us to work up to, and like all ideal standards will never be reached, but will always exert its pull on our hearts and minds. And what authority: 'Follow thou me'! Who ever spoke like that!"

This was written to Margaret on 23 January 1942, and two weeks later, on 11 February, a letter followed to tell her that he was also reading T. R. Glover's book *The Disciple* which was published in 1941 and which she had sent him. He found it a very pleasant book. Glover, with his knowledge of the Graeco-Roman world, throws a good many sidelights on the New Testament story.

"To me the marvel is the intense passion and fire that there was in that movement, and remained in it for so long. Seeley in his *Ecce Homo* talks of the 'enthusiasm of humanity' as the keynote of the mission of Jesus. But 'enthusiasm' is a poor word for that intensity of spirit that moved people's souls. It was more like the burning bush, which never was consumed as described in Exodus in the Bible.

"The love of God for man and all that it implied and set going was certainly the most enormous force that has ever been released in human affairs. And in the centre of this fire stands the calm, quiet figure of Jesus in all his majestic authority. He seemed to set everybody round Him on fire while He himself remains at perfect peace – the centre of quiet in a raging tornado. Paul's letters prove how men were roused and moved and fired to their inmost depths."

46

Smuts applied this vision of Jesus as the messenger of God to the reform of the modern world, including South Africa, as I will show in my chapter on the New South Africa.

The amazing part of all this study and analysis of the outlook and the personality of Jesus and the numerous letters Smuts wrote about his conclusions is that they took place during the height of the Second World War when the outcome of the immense struggle hung in the balance. Smuts at the time was 72 years old and in his letter to Margaret on 10 March 1942 he openly complained that he had spent three most gruelling days in the South African Parliament, fighting his departmental estimates as prime minister and minister of defence through the House, in the teeth of most violent opposition. All the time the heavy war works had to be dealt with, while serious internal problems arising from war conditions had to be attended to with the usual paraphernalia of deputations and interviews galore.

"I sometimes sit back and think what is it that makes an old man like me, whose heart and head are in quite another world, continue untiringly and unrestingly in tasks like these. It is a question not so easy to answer. We are curious mixtures in which the high and the low curiously blend and we deceive ourselves if we put it all to the credit of our virtue or good qualities.

"There is a good deal of the devil also in it. There is an elemental drive which will not give in to opposition, and sometimes uses the same weapons with which the opponents fight. But I do flatter myself that behind it all is a deeper faith and loyalty to what is good and really worth fighting for. But oh, how tired one gets of the unending effort and toil!

"I can understand the case of those monarchs in history who as they passed their prime voluntarily retired to seclusion and meditation or enjoyments of the flesh. I could retire to the enjoyments of the spirit and the mind, if I could honourably let go, but I can't. It is a case of bondage to the ideal, to the light one is compelled to follow, whatever the cost. Determinism and free will join hands here and in being a slave one is really free. Such is our human lot, and so the temporal and the eternal join hands in shaping our course through this world, which is yet so much more than this world. Well, keep well and cheerful and after all life is not so bad or so hard," was his cheery farewell to Margaret.

Not long after this, Margaret and Smuts as followers of Jesus were severely tested on the issue of violence and the use of force and military might as the supreme instrument of war. Margaret as a Quaker was against the War policy. To make matters worse, she was also chairperson of the regional quarterly meetings of the Society of Friends, as the Quakers are officially known. As such, in 1942, when the Second World War was at its most decisive phase she had to write a minute (a report) for the quarterly meeting.

In her desperation and uncertainty as to how to write her report she wrote to her friend Jan about her difficulties in regard to the problem of war as it concerned sincere Friends and of her difficulties in composing the minute.

Smuts replied to her, on 7 June 1942 stating that he felt the tragedy of the situation as did any Friend, "and I do believe that under ideal conditions the Christian message is the only answer to our difficulties".

Then he went on to explain: "But, of course, the situation for Jesus was much simplified by the existence of the omnipotent Roman Empire, and by his sound principle of leaving to Caesar what was Caesar's. We on the other hand are in the position of Caesar, responsible for peace and war, for the maintenance of social order against brute violence and aggression. Ours is therefore a much more complex situation than that which Jesus had to face.

"What would He have done in Caesar's place and faced with a ruthless attack on the values which man's age long endeavour had laboriously accomplished? Is that not a very different position from that which the Gospel envisages? Is that not the position of old man Blake where he says: 'I shall not cease from mortal strife, nor shall my sword sleep in my hand', etc. I do believe that this is not mere poetic imagery, but the true heroic attitude, and that it is in the ultimate spirit of Christ.

"The passive defeatist view of Jesus does him no justice. He did not spare Himself in the cause of right, and would not have spared anybody if called to maintain the right. The true Christians are those in all lands who by prayer and endurance where possible, and by heroic self-sacrifice and battling where that is possible, stand up for the right as they see it and refuse to knuckle under to wrong.

"The heroic Christ is to me the real Christ, and the passive acquiescence in omnipotent wrong is to me a negation of all that He stands for."

Jan must have realised that this explanation of the "heroic Christ" and the acceptance of force and war would shock and upset Margaret. He therefore ended his letter by telling her that he looked forward to her minute. "You must not look upon the above as condemnation in advance. I only feel that the wars of the spirit may not and are not sufficient if evil has to be routed in this practical world. Carnal weapons must be used if necessary! Goodnight, Jan."

And then only two weeks and two days later, before Margaret even had time to reply, Jan wrote one of his most dramatic letters on the meaning of tragedy, not only as portrayed in Shakespeare's well-known and terrible tragedies, but also in the agony of Jesus and his tragic sacrifice on the Cross. It is to my mind one of the most awe-inspiring, yet sublime and dramatic revelations of Smuts's analysis of the personality of Jesus.

In this letter of 23 June 1942, at one of the most critical phases of the Second World War after the capture of Tobruk by Rommel in North Africa and the immense battles in Russia, Churchill had rushed to Washington to confer with President Roosevelt, while Smuts held conferences at Libertas in Pretoria with a large and distinguished company to plan future strategies in North Africa, Madagascar and other theatres of the worldwide war.

"The future of man is the stakes for which we are contending and one cannot give too much thought to the right lines for our world-wide strategy. Of course I cannot here discuss what my views are although I am sure you would both be interested."

He also told her that "with this large and distinguished company at Libertas I had no free time, and had to dock my hours of sleep for drafting documents and thinking out plans. But even so I found some sleepless midnight moments to read Raleigh's little book on Shakespeare."

He was referring to Sir Walter Alexander Raleigh's *Shakespeare* which had appeared in 1907, a copy of which Margaret had sent him. He informed her that he was especially interested in Raleigh's point that those terrible tragedies, such as Macbeth, Lear, Othello and others, which one can scarcely bear to read in their concentrated horror, must have racked the very soul of Shakespeare in the process of writing them and brought his mind to the very verge of insanity.

"I had never thought of this aspect. But of course it must be so. You cannot in imagination work out those awful problems of human fate without being shaken to your very foundations. And another point Sir Walter Raleigh makes is that in the white heat of sacrifice even the worst crimes are transmuted and become sublime and awe-inspiring in a way which makes you quite forget the crime. Thus Othello's murder of his wife because of his passionate love. Human nature in its peak moments passes beyond good and evil, and becomes almost godlike in spite of the breach of the moral law. I suppose that is why the ancients looked upon madness as divine."

Smuts then applied these thoughts in the middle of that dramatic night to the person of Jesus. "How much more godlike must be the high passion and sacrifice when the object is itself the highest. Think of Jesus, conscious that He is the Messiah elect, going up to Jerusalem to suffer those horrors and agonies which He so clearly forebodes! His is surely the greatest drama in all history. And what must have passed through that great soul in those last days, when his disciples didn't understand Him, his own people hated Him to death and He was only upborne by his high resolve and sacrifice. And then came a moment at the end when He thought that even God had forsaken Him. What a drama!

"And then a woman, a woman He had saved from shipwreck, in her blinding love, saw that vision of Him which became the resurrection and the foundation of the Christian order. His sacrifice did force the Kingdom of God, but not in the way He had thought, but through that vision born of love and tears."

Here Smuts with his fine knowledge of English poetry was quoting from Hartley Coleridge's well-known poem "Nultum Dilexit" in which he wrote:

> She sat and wept beneath His feet; the weight
> Of sin oppressed her heart . . .
> I am a sinner, full of doubts and fears,
> Make me a humble thing of love and tears.

Smuts called this the highlight of tragedy, surpassing anything that even the imagination of Shakespeare could encompass.

He pointed out that it was not the Virgin Mary who thus became the Mother of Christianity but Mary Magdalene, who in the Bible is also described as the woman of Magdala, a town near Tiberias on the western shore of the Sea of Galilee.

In the Bible dictionary she is named as the Mary out of whom seven devils were cast out. According to Luke 8:2 she then followed Jesus. When Jesus was crucified she was near Him, according to Matthew 27:56. Both Mark and John also mention this in their gospels. She then attended the burial of Jesus, according to Matthew and Mark, and visited the tomb in the morning when Jesus appeared to her, according to Mark and John.

It was through this first vision of the risen Christ that Mary Magdalene became the Mother of the Christian faith and the Christian church. Smuts mentions this in his letter and adds: "But Jesus stands out even beyond that as the very God. I think that is the nearest to the godlike we can ever and shall ever come and we do right in bowing before Him in worship and adoration."

He told Margaret in his letter that all this was borne in on him that dramatic night when he was reading Raleigh on Shakespeare's tragedies. "And is not Mary a lovely character, lovely beyond anything in Shakespeare's wonderful women! I think she must have been the Mary who anointed Him with fragrant oil and dried his feet with her dear hair. At least I hope so.

"These colourful ways of the East express what is lovely in life much better than our restraints and inhibitions. How wonderful are these high moments of life! And they come in the most humble surroundings and commonplace circumstances. What could be more lowly and modest than the primitive Galilean society where these mighty wonders of human nature were wrought? How much greater and more wonderful than anything in the experience of the mighty contemporary Tiberius or the philosophy of the contemporary Seneca. At least I think they were contemporaries of Jesus."

Here Smuts was right. Both the mighty Roman emperor Tiberius and the well-known Roman stoic philosopher, dramatist and statesman, Lucus Annaeus Seneca were contemporaries of Jesus. Tiberius was born in 42 B.C. and died in A.D. 37 after he became emperor in A.D. 14. Seneca was born in 3 B.C. and died in A.D. 65.

In his letter of 10 July 1942 to Margaret he reverted to the last

51

phase of the life of Jesus on earth. He was especially interested in the mystery of how Jesus put his ideas and his vision across to those simple folk of his time. Socrates had the advantage of the greatest literary craftsman of all time to paint his immortal picture (here refering to Plato who immortalised Socrates's method of philosophic questioning). But the tales of these simple folk, with their primitive language, were like the story-telling of children. And yet the result was so immensely impressive, not even a Shakespeare could have done that last phase of the Master better, and the heroic simplicity of it all became so telling that one could scarcely bear to read it.

"The great figure in all his sorrow and faith, the disciples milling around, the women standing afar, the priests in their hour, the governor in his defeat, the stranger from Africa who bears the cross, the darkness, the sorrowing, sobbing women at the tomb, the vision of Magdalene through her tears, and her final cry: Rabboni; the joyful running back, the spreading of the Vision; the passing away in glory in the clouds."

To Smuts all this was described in the simplest language of a child's fairy tale – and yet it had a tremendous effect on one's mind. How much of it got across? Perhaps even more in some respects than was there; in other respects so much less.

"The whole thing looks like a miracle of human nature and experience." And yet always the impression remained that the truth was greater than the story, and that there was something far greater in that tragedy than the pen had conveyed.

"There are indeed two mysteries: the one is the Master, Jesus, the other is the disciples whose weakness could convey and accomplish so much. Surely there must be something godlike in man, and both the Master and his disciples are a proof of that fact. There is a revelation of spirit which makes us see into the depths of the spirit which lies embedded in our mortal clay."

This was written at the most critical period of the Second World War, when the outcome was very much in the balance. Smuts was deeply worried and in this frame of mind he concentrated his thoughts on the power and personality of Jesus the miracle worker, the Son of God. Jesus was his guiding star, the power that kept him going and which inspired him to believe in final victory over the evil forces of Nazism.

It was at about this time, in 1943 or 1944, that he was confidentially informed, probably by Churchill, of the possibility of the atom bomb which was being constructed in the USA.

This, as well as the German reverses in Russia and some improvement in the general war situation, must have restored his self-confidence. The tone of his letters to Margaret became somewhat different, with a little less direct appeal to God and the power and personality of Jesus.

Towards the end of the Second World War in 1944 he saw victory approaching and on 14 November 1944 he poured out his heart to his old friend Chaim Weizmann, the famous chemist who became a respected Zionist leader.

"Victory is approaching and can now not be far off. But it will dawn over a bleak world, bled white with the loss of life and treasure beyond anything in the history of the race. I am a firm believer in man – as I am in God – but I must admit that the prospect before the world, even with victory, appals me." But he hoped that the genius of his race, which had accomplished so much in the past, would enable mankind to survive and surmount the dangers then facing them even in the hour of victory.

To his friend Margaret in the final hour of victory he was more positive in his faith in God, in the Son Jesus and even in man. On 21 January 1945 he referred in his letter to her to the foreword he had written to Dr. Robert Broom's new book on the Sterkfontein and Kromdraai apemen who evidently lived in the great pluvials in Southern Africa millions of years ago.

This set his mind and his pen going. "Think of our human march from those ancient times – a million years ago if not more – up to today, with all our achievements in science, art and religion! Need we despair of the future, in the mess which troubles our human affairs today?

"Is there not something Godlike in us, in spite of all the devilries which are clogging our progress, like this war and the other social failures which surround us? Man is a revelation of the Divine. God reveals himself not only in the supreme characters of our race – in the Son and sons of God – but also in the human average, slowly rising beyond and above the sordid animal origins which we have not yet outlived. Man shows what Nature is capable of under favourable conditions. The foundations of the Divine are revealed by the footprints of man in prehistory. And so prehistory becomes a witness to the Divine character of this universe as a whole."

CHAPTER FIVE

Holism of the spirit

I have already mentioned that, four years after the publication of his *Holism and Evolution*, Smuts was anxious to write a sequel to explain the impact of his theory of holism on the spiritual issues of life. At the time (1929) he realised that his first book had been based on inadequate and somewhat outdated scientific knowledge prior to the tremendous transformations brought about by both Einstein's theory of relativity and the quantum theory.

In 1931 he was president of the British Association for the Advancement of Science and as such delivered the presidential address at its centenary celebrations in September 1931. The main import of his address was to get an answer to the insistent question in scientific and philosophic circles: How has value become a reality?

In his official biography of Smuts Professor Hancock points out that when Smuts in his presidential address sketched the outlines of an answer to this important question he also announced the theme of his second book on holism of the spirit.

The universe Smuts had depicted in his first book was structural in each of its successive evolutionary forms. The new science had since revealed that life and the higher values which emerged from this belonged to the same structural order.

He explained it as follows: "The free creativeness of mind is possible because as we have seen, the world ultimately consists, not of material stuff but of patterns, of organisation, the evolution of which evolves no absolute creation of an alien world of material from nothing.

"The purely structural character of reality thus helps to render possible and intelligible the free creativeness of life and mind, and accounts for the unlimited wealth of fresh patterns which the mind

55

freely creates on the basis of the existing physical patterns. The highest reach of this creative process is seen in the realm of values."

This was Smuts, the statesman-philosopher-scientist relating at speed and in vivid prose his story of the evolving cosmic structure of the universe from the curves of space-time to the emergence of man with his higher values linking him to the Divine.

Smuts, the scientist, the creator of holism, was talking to 2 000 fellow-scientists who at the end of his presidential address gave him a standing ovation, a signal honour to their former Boer War enemy. So true and remarkable his insight and interpretation of scientific reality were regarded at the time that in 1964, 33 years later, eight out of ten scientists approached still regarded his presidential address of 1931 as scientifically accurate and outstanding.

It was on the basis of his scientific insight in 1931 that he wanted to write his second book on holism, combining science and spiritual values to reveal to mankind holism of the spirit.

Smuts, however, realised that before he could write about science and religion and apply his holistic theory to the realms of spiritual issues, he had better brush up on his study of the Bible and especially the New Testament. So in 1937 he started with a systematic study of the Greek New Testament.

As had been his custom since 1919, he explained his plans to his friend Margaret Clark Gillett in a letter of 3 April 1937.

"I have recently taken to reading the New Testament again in Greek, partially to recover some of my half-forgotten Greek, but especially to see whether I can now get some fresh light on the Gospel story. We have put such a thick varnish of glosses and interpretations on the original account that a special effort has to be made to get back the simple intentions of the original authors.

"So I am once more re-reading the wonderful story and have now done most of Matthew. I can only do a small bit each night. When I have done all four Gospels I shall try to clarify my mind and see whether any fresh conclusions are possible. When last I read the Greek Testament it was with very orthodox eyes, which I have no longer. And yet I am probably today more deeply interested to get at its meaning than I was in my orthodox youth." What profoundly interested Smuts at this period of his life was the utter simplicity of the story of Jesus as described by the apostles, none of whom were men of great learning. Yet the detail and the vividness of the Gospel stories amazed him. He could hardly believe, yet did believe, that there had been, once upon a time, an order of existence where simple men walked the earth filled with the Spirit, however poor in earthly things they were. Even more amazing was that they were primitive peasants.

In a letter to Margaret on 8 October 1937 he told her that he was deeply sorry that he could not be in Cape Town when she was there. It would have been good for them to have climbed Table Mountain. "To me Table Mountain is not just sticks and stones and things [a phrase in proverbial use among the Gilletts] but a deep living experience wherein spirit holds converse with spirit, and time and space form no barriers but fresh means of contact. We enter through this visible means into the invisible world within them. As the German poet Goethe wrote: 'All things transitory are but a symbol of Love's diviner being'."

It was at this time, around 1937, that he was very anxious to write his *Holism of the Spirit* on the basis of his profound interest in the personality of Jesus. For a time he surrendered himself to his investigations but the rise of Hitler and the threat of war and revolutions disturbed his quiet contemplation and his ability to express his deepest thoughts. He later realised that war was inevitable, and with his sensitive nature he felt that mankind had once again lost its anchorage and was driven this way and that way by fanatical ideologies and false Messiahs. He asked himself what the prospects were for a Christian recovery to restore the bonds between God and Man.

Although in this pre-war period the New Testament still fascinated him, he found no direct answers to the political problems of his time. He realised too that when Jesus had lived nineteen centuries ago the Roman Empire safeguarded the then world government. Jesus had lived within the shelter of the Roman peace and had no experience of the problems of power.

But now in 1938-9 Hitler, supported by Mussolini and Japan, threatened world peace. Smuts was made prime minister of South Africa and declared war on Germany and Italy. He decided that his own faith must be militant to resist evil to the uttermost. On 7 September 1939 Churchill telegraphed him: "I rejoice to feel that we are once again on commando together."

57

Right from the start, Smuts regarded the war in essence as a large human and spiritual conflict. He realised too that he would have no time or opportunity to write *Holism II*, but he continued his interest in matters of the spirit.

In a letter on 22 December 1939 to his American friend Florence Lamont he wrote: "I believe in the Spirit which has led humanity on, and blossomed in all the great ideas which underlie our Western culture. The things Hitler stands for are the negation of all this, and if Nazism is a crusade, no less is that greater Crusade of the Spirit on which we have set out.

"Victory is not guaranteed us; the Right oftener than not is defeated. But still the Spirit beckons and leads us on. It is the Divine which shapes our course through the world. Bacon has said that the human mind moves upon the poles of truth."

Francis Bacon in his *Essays* wrote: "Certainly, it is heaven upon earth, to have a man's mind turn on the poles of truth." To this Smuts added: "And equally truly it may be said that man follows the best and highest, even when it appears most hard to attain."

It was at this time in 1939 and 1940, when Hitler had a number of swift military victories, that Smuts in his private life and letter-writing to his friends revealed his most intense concentration on matters of the spirit. In the long letter to Margaret on 24 January 1940, quoted in Chapter 4, he also wrote:

"The Roman Empire . . . went because, or rather while, decent cultured people accepted their fate and cultivated their little gardens of culture while the weeds (of barbarism) spread around them until their gardens were also invaded and submerged. Both acquiescence and vain expectation are dangerous. But what practicable middle course is there?

"Perhaps we shall have to proceed step by step, guided by practical experience, in the English way, and so grope forward to the light and truth."

Is this not also a wise recommendation for our modern world and especially for the problems of southern Africa?

As if this were not sufficient spiritual advice given to Margaret in January 1940, two months later on Sunday, 3 March 1940, another revelation of his soul followed after breakfast:

"It is a perfect morning; wind, cold and heat gone, the doves in the oaks, the little squirrels dart about like arrows. This morning I awoke with pleasant thoughts of my friends as from a dream, and so I turned once more to Paul's great Hymn of love with its high poetry and higher spirituality.

"At breakfast I said I had been reading 1 Corinthians 13 in Greek, and then (to my envy) Isie, my wife, started repeating the chapter in Greek, saying that this was the only chapter in the New Testament she could say in that tongue.

"There is something indefinable in the New Testament that often carries me clean off my feet, and this chapter is outstanding even in that book of the soul. It is not so much religion as something deeper that touches all the secret springs of life. The whole theory of perception is transformed by that wonderful line: 'Now we see in a mirror – in an aenigma (Greek for enigma); then we shall see face to face.' This is the higher Realism. Now we shall know in parts; then we shall know the whole. When the perfect comes the imperfect (the way of the partial) goes."

Smuts then quoted three Greek words in the original Greek script. These are translated as faith, hope and love. He calls them "these three" and asks: "Has anybody ever summed up the depths of the human soul in simpler and more effective terms? I look upon the New Testament as the spiritual highlight of the human race. No insight since, no expression since of the human soul in its highest and noblest phases, has equalled the vision and expression of it given in the New Testament.

"And so with all our science, all our wider world view of today, we still say, 'Thank God for Jesus and his testament of Love'. I can sit and think of those incomparable passages with my body literally in a quiver. The great poets do not affect me like that, except when now and then (as in Blake or Whitman) they but re-echo the music of the New Testament.

"To me the spiritual inspiration of that age remains a great mystery. How is it that at that time of all times there was such a flowering out of the human soul in noblest vision and expression? And how have we fallen from that vision since? But, whatever the relapse, the union itself remains the abiding possession of the race. It is but a vision.

"That wonderful transfiguration on the Mountain which came to Jesus and his three disciples was but a vision revealed in a supreme exhaltation of the spirit. But is it not as true and real as the most solid things that we see with our eyes or touch with our hands? Does the Soul-Unison not take us face to face with Reality? We look for facts, but in the world of the Spirit are there not higher realities than so-called facts? Facts are precious, but they are still of the parts, the details, whereas the Vision is the whole, face to face with the Real, so far as one can ever know the real."

On the question of immortality, he wrote in his letter to Margaret of 7 April 1940: "It is difficult to conceive of all life being conserved in its individual form for all eternity. For if the souls of men, why not the souls of every living creature; and is matter itself not a lower form of life?"

Smuts wrote that this universal conservation not only appalled him, but that it was also contrary to the most recent developments in science, which has done away with the conservation both of energy and matter. Here he refers to the quantum theory which at that time gave a new insight into our physical world.

He followed this up by explaining that there was a suspense account labelled "mystery" in all our human knowledge, and personal immortality may be an item in that account. This reminded him of George Eliot's idea in her lines: "O may I join the choir invisible – the company of all who have in life contributed to the better and higher order of the future and leave it at that. I can conceive my dear friends going and my living on and cherishing their sweet memory until I too go."

It was a pity that Smuts at this period could not find the time to complete his second book on holism, as it is evident from his volumi- nous letter-writing about Jesus and on spiritual issues in general that he was constantly reading and thinking about religion and the power of the spirit. He came nearest to unravelling the deeper insight and explaining the great mystery of holism as the indwelling spirit and the outward expression of this mysterious universe in his letter of 9 May 1940 to Margaret.

He told her that a dreary night debate was going on in Parliament, so he was able to use the time to drop her a line. The book on S. Alexander, *Philosophical and Literary Pieces* (1939) had arrived and he had some free night hours to read it. He found Alexander a queer old boy, combining a whimsical simplicity with much worldly wisdom and profound metaphysics. Like many other thinkers of the day, he approached holism without seeing it as a landmark in human thought.

To him it was clear that Alexander, with his metaphysics, was jealous of Whitehead whose star was rising in philosophy. But he need not have been, for all metaphysics of today is but a phase, passing like all the effort of our time of rapid transition. "Not in these noises," as Milton said, "will the new philosophy be written." "We do but see in a glass darkly", as Paul expressed it in 1 Corinthians 13, verse 12, "the shape of things to come", to quote from H.G. Wells's book *The Shape of Things to Come*.

Then Smuts went on to explain that modern thinkers must transcend the Hebraic deity which modern science had created. "We must fuse the conceptions of the divine and the human. What was dimly foreseen in the Christian incarnation must be experienced in a more adequate form, and shorn of its imagery.

"The universe must be seen as the organic structure that it is: instinct with divinity, big with the inner spirit which is shaping and creating it, and of which it is but the progressive expression. 'The Divine vision still was seen – and Jesus still the Form was thine,' as old Blake put it in the language of our childhood." (This is a quotation from William Blake's poem "Jerusalem".)

Smuts then continued: "I sometimes feel my own conception trembling on the brink of this vision. It is the holism of the spirit which is at once the indwelling spirit and the outward expression of this mysterious universe. But there is something warm and near and intimate about it, which can only be expressed in the category of personality with the complexity of the physical universe.

"It is so difficult to realise and formulate in thought the truth that that vast Other, not myself, is yet not really alien or different, but the other of myself. The Universal is incarnate in the particular. The universe and the soul are like body and soul in the human individual. The Infinite is the unit. I suppose we shall yet succeed in getting harmony among our intuitions and concepts but at present there are still deep gulfs dividing them. But the reconciliation will come."

At this crucial time in the Second World War when Hitler and his cohorts were reaping huge victories, Smuts turned 70 on 24 May 1940. He was still immensely active on a wide front, fit and trim, and as L.S. Amery wrote to him from Whitehall, "Everyone tells me that the great issues of the day in South Africa and in the world have rejuvenated you out of all recognition. Well, more power to your elbow, or perhaps I should say to your keen brain and strong will; for we shall need all the help we can get if civilisation is to survive."

He was at this stage of his life even more enamoured by the quantum theory and the theory of wave mechanics which had revolutionised science and introduced the new genetic, organic and holistic principle whereby, in his words, the "universe consisted not only of electrons and radiations but also of souls and aspirations".

When both Arthur and Margaret wrote to him from the Cottswolds where they were visiting he waxed lyrical about the new atomic science of wave mechanics in his reply of 14 June 1940:

"I hope there will be great peace and refreshment for you both. How blessed the great rhythms of nature are to the soul! For according to atomic physics the great enduring masses of the earth – mountains and all solid things – are essentially nothing but continuous rhythmical repetitions of the wave mechanics which is matter. An atom is just a continuous repetition of a particular set of electronic waves or pulsations. And the Cottswold hills but a grand symphony of such rhythmical waves. Looking at the earth, its hills and mountains, is in essence the same as history to a continuous musical symphony, only with a more monotonous soothing series of notes. Matter is really the frozen music of the universe.

"And what a peace, a consolation, appeasement of mind and eye there is in that solemn frozen music, whose winding rhythms are constituted by the pleasing outlines and contours of hill and dale. As the ear hears one kind of music, so the eye is enchanted by this more massive music of the earth.

"God to whom there is no distinction of ear and eye, enjoys it all in his infinite bliss. Perhaps when we have shifted off this mortal coil, as Shakespeare wrote in *Hamlet*, with its differentiated senses we shall also hear that universal music which we now see as matter."

It was at this time, at the beginning of 1941, that I joined Smuts as an information officer in his government in Pretoria and Cape Town. As a Rhodes Scholar at Oxford I had written a thesis on state and culture under the supervision of Professor R.B. Collingwood, one of the foremost professors of Philosophy at the time. I was awarded the B.Litt. degree for this thesis which was later converted to an M. Litt.

When I left Oxford in 1936 Professor Collingwood suggested that when I returned to South Africa I should follow up my research on Smuts's holism. He explained that there was something worthwhile in his theory, but that "we don't know exactly what it is and we need someone to research it and explain it". I was naturally flattered that I had been selected to fulfil this task, and after I returned to South Africa I wrote to Smuts about it.

He promised to see me and it was agreed that we should meet sometime in 1939, but when Hitler started his military manoeuvres and conquests Smuts became involved in international efforts to stop him and our appointment was cancelled.

I had meanwhile returned to journalism and was writing a daily column on the international situation for a big Afrikaans daily, *Die Vaderland*, in Johannesburg. General J.B.M. Hertzog, twice prime minister of South Africa, was the chairman of the company controlling the paper and often complimented me on my articles.

But after war broke out and I predicted that Hitler, in spite of all his spectacular victories, would eventually lose the war, the position changed. In 1941 Hertzog was indisposed and Oswald Pirow, the former minister of defence in his government became the acting chairman. He was of German descent and an active supporter of Hitler.

Pretty soon the editor of *Die Vaderland*, Mr Willem van Heerden, and I were summoned to Pretoria to appear before Pirow who immediately wanted to know from me why I predicted almost daily that Hitler would lose the war.

When I told him that Germany in spite of her initial victories did not have the resources for a long war and that Hitler would be crushed, Pirow revealed that he, as the previous minister of defence, had visited Hitler and had been taken to Spain during the Spanish war to acquaint himself with the new German tactics of hammering a breach into the enemy lines, penetrating them and fanning out behind the front. Pirow told me that these tactics were so successful that no enemy could resist Hitler who on that basis would win the war.

He gave me instructions to announce the next day in my column that Hitler would win the war. When I told him I could not do so he threatened to fire me, whereupon I immediately resigned my position on the paper.

That same afternoon I sent word to General Smuts and informed him of the events leading up to my resignation and offering my services to him. The next day he sent Mr A. N. Wilson, the then director of information, to me and offered me a job as an information officer on his staff.

This was the turning point in my life, the fulfilment of my desire to work closely with Smuts and the beginning of my intense study and research into his personality, his holism, his romantic attachment to a number of women and eventually also into his deep interest in religion and the influence of Jesus Christ on his outlook.

For the next nine years I worked closely with Smuts, first as an information officer and later as the editor in chief of five of his Afrikaans political newspapers, and was able to observe his vitality and to experience his active and comprehensive brain at first hand. One of the highlights of this association came in 1946 when I was with him at Flushing Meadows, outside New York, where he played a leading role in the formation of the United Nations, instituted to safeguard the future peace of the world. There he introduced me to Harry S. Truman, the American president who ended the Second World War by dropping two atomic bombs onto the Japanese cities of Nagasaki and Hiroshima.

President Truman took a great liking to me because my father and his brothers had taken part in the battles of the Anglo-Boer War and he, as a youngster in the United States at the time, had taken a great interest in the war, followed the outcome of the battles in the American newspapers and always had the desire to visit the historic battlefields. He was astonished that I had never seen them, and made me promise to visit them on my return to South Africa and send him full reports. He also invited me to visit him if and when I was in the United States, and this I did on several occasions.

Being with Smuts and working closely with him was the fulfilment of my life's ambition, but if I had hoped that this would also open to me the door to his inner mind and introduce me to the mysteries of his holistic outlook and his personal thoughts, I was sadly mistaken. I soon found out that he resented it when I asked personal questions about his life, his religion and his association with women.

On several occasions when I tried to intrude in his personal life, he dismissed me peremptorily. I was naturally disappointed and at the time did not know that, although he was averse to talking to me about his inner life, he put it all in writing in letters to his friends almost every night. Only later, after his death in 1950, was a book in the form of seven volumes of personal letters written over more than sixty years and revealing his inner thoughts and beliefs available to students of his life.

At about this time, Margaret sent him two books on religion, Albert Schweitzer's book on *The Mysticism of the Apostle Paul* and A.C. Bradley's *Ideals of Religion*, which he read at night when the Second World War was at its most intense.

In thanking her for the books, Smuts told her that he was still looking for the God within us, based on Jesus' text that "the kingdom of heaven is among you".

He then went on to explain: "I believe if we could see rightly and think clearly, we could see that in us which represents the common root of God and man, the point of incarnation, so to say, in our personality. Great souls sense that divine within, but of course transpose it to something objective without – and so the immanent becomes the transcendent. But this immanent is really not ourselves; it is something more than the individual asset.

"It is also the point where the individual and the universe meet – in some other form of incarnation. The God which is my soul is really not myself, but something far more universal, whose dwelling is the light of setting suns as William Wordsworth wrote in his beautiful poem: 'Lines composed a few miles above Tintern Abbey', and not merely my poor body."

Smuts wondered whether Margaret and her husband, Arthur, followed this simple line of his thoughts – "simple and yet going to the very roots of religion and philosophy and much besides which is great within us. This is the Source, in us, and yet more than us, just as love is in us, and yet fills the universe."

At this point in his life he was afraid that these letters "with their divagations into side issues must be boring to you", as he wrote to Margaret, but then he explained that "the letters just flow from an uncontrollable pen as I write".

After that his letters on religion and spiritual issues seem to dry up for some time. He became more interested in writing about philosophy to Princess Frederica of Greece, although he still continued his weekly letters to Margaret. And when Frederica came to stay in Cape Town the Greek princesses lunched daily with him at Libertas – "they are great fun and splendid company", and to crown it all Frederica became a student of holism.

Smuts became even more enamoured of the Greek crown princess and took her with him on a flight to Nairobi and after that to Cairo. On the way back he arranged with his pilot to fly over the Victoria Falls, as Frederica was anxious to see this famous tourist attraction. In all this excitement he was not sure whether he had written his weekly letter to Margaret or forgotten it that week. What is even more interesting is that he devoted his letter of 26 December 1942, shortly after his flight across Africa with Frederica, to a lengthy discussion of evil.

Margaret in her previous letter to him speculated about God and his changeable character at different times and different circumstances. In his reply on 26 December he told her that he was reading Fausset's book on Walt Whitman. From this he had discovered for the first time that Whitman was not quite normal in his sexual make-up and had homosexual leanings, "which I might have inferred from his poem 'Calamus' but did not infer in my simplicity and ignorance of such abnormalities. This is all valuable stuff in a way, unknown to me when I wrote about him.

"Whitman did a great service to me in making me appreciate the Natural man and freeing me from much theological or conventional preconceptions due to my early pious upbringing. It was a sort of liberation, as St Paul was liberated from the Law and its damnations by his Damascus vision.

"Sin ceased to dominate my view of life, and this was a great release as I was inclined to be severely puritanical in all things. A great release and a useful service."

This was indeed an interesting confession coming from such a famous world leader as Field Marshal Jan Smuts was at this stage of world history. He went on to explain how this had affected his estimation of Walt Whitman in his later years and from deeper thought and experience of realities. He then came to the conclusion that there was much more in the earlier views than Whitman ever understood or at least put in his poems.

"You do not reach your full human stature by reverting to the natural or biological man but by moving onward and making a higher synthesis of the old and the new in experience, by appreciating the dreadful reality of evil and not shutting one's eyes to it, and by rising

66

from the experience of our limitations, our weaknesses and flaws to a deeper conception of the real human.

"Experience is really the stepping-stone by which we rise to this higher self as Alfred Tennyson expressed in his poem 'In Memoriam': 'That men may rise on stepping-stones of their dead selves to higher things'."

Smuts was convinced that only in this process can peace and harmony be attained by the individual and not by reverting to the earlier, purely natural phase. "There is this much in the orthodox view, and it means a deeper reading of the problem of life. Good and evil are realities to be squarely faced, and we do not get at the real thing by ignoring or glossing over evil.

"In a very true sense the Human-Divine is based on this deeper experience and on the synthesis arising from such experience."

Smuts then went on to explain that Whitman, according to his biographer Fausset, had made the same mistake in his view of democratic man, who also is not the last word, but has to learn to rise above the shortcomings of a crude democracy and the evils of the competitive society in order to form that society or brotherhood of men which is the next stage in our social and communal progress.

In both cases, both in regard to our individual lives and in our social and democratic relationships, we move from the natural to the spiritual level in our holistic rise, as Smuts explained Fausset's conception. He added, however, that Fausset never used his holistic ideas as he was probably not aware of the concept of holism which Smuts had originated after his time.

Smuts assumed that it was really Whitman who had influenced Fausset to make this move from the natural to the spiritual level. He understood him in that sense, and thought him an illustration of personal holism (as well as holism of the spirit).

However, Smuts later obtained fuller biographical material on Whitman and realised (and announced in his letter) that he had been wrong in this assumption. He explained it fully to Margaret in his previously quoted letter of 26 December 1942 as follows:

"It is a curious but profoundly true fact that the higher integration is only reached through experience of the lower, that is in a way almost blasphemous to say, the higher good incorporates the evil we have done and passed through, and that the highest does not negate so much

67

as absorb and incorporate the lower and the lowest.

"Evil becomes an ingredient in the final good which we attain on the higher synthesis or integration of life. Holism seems to imply this deeper spiritual view of the universe. Evil is not extrinsic to it, but, in some way difficult to comprehend, natural to it and a constituent element in it. The great lesson of experience is to absorb, transmute and sublimate evil and make it an element to enrich, rather than a dominant factor to dominate life."

He then explained to Margaret, as I have already mentioned, that she, as was apparent in her previous letter to him, also had some strange speculations about God and His changeable character in different circumstances. I shall refer to this in my next chapter when I discuss God and the new physics as well as Smuts's views of God in the light of his holism in nature as well as in the world of the spirit.

From my contact with General Smuts in 1942 and 1943 when I was working for him and could observe him at close quarters, as well as in my subsequent research into his life, I am convinced that a fundamental change came in his life at this stage. This was due to the interaction of four factors or developments which forced him finally to give up his intention to write *Holism of the Spirit* as a sequel to his first book, *Holism and Evolution*.

Although old age never worried him or affected his vitality, he reached 72 and 73 years at a time when the Second World War was at its most crucial stage. He was not only carrying impossible burdens in South Africa where he was constantly being attacked by a determined opposition, but he was also under pressure in the wider war situation where urgent calls were made on him to fulfil important duties and take vital decisions in view of Winston Churchill's illness with pneumonia and the fact that President Franklin D. Roosevelt, with his sick body, was also forced to overstrain himself by carrying impossible burdens.

In his letter to Margaret on 23 February 1942 he referred to his great worry and anxiety for both Churchill and Roosevelt. He was always terrified that he would suddenly and unexpectedly hear of their breakdown under strain. And to complicate matters even further, "poor Gandhi chose this moment to run for suicide as the way out" by his ill-fated decision at the age of 73 to begin a twenty-one days' fast in a British jail in Poona where he was being detained. Gandhi's son

Manilal phoned and wired from Durban to ask Smuts to send him by plane to the Aga Khan's palace at Poona, or to let him talk by telephone to his father or other relatives.

Smuts told Margaret that he had agreed to Manilal's request but he did not know if this would pass the censor in India. "It is such a pitiable end – to try and change men's minds by a sort of moral blackmail. But there is always something peculiarly disagreeable in the Gandhi technique, much as I honour and respect him for his great qualities." In my last chapter I shall enlarge on the strange relationship between Smuts and Gandhi.

And to complicate Smuts's life and work further, Princess Frederica turned up during this worrying time to try to persuade him to use his influence with Churchill and Roosevelt and the other Allied leaders to restore the Greek throne once Greece was liberated. Smuts, who liked the princess a great deal, unlike Churchill who saw her as a German Hohenzollern granddaughter of the Kaiser, was rather pleased with her visit and entertained her and her royal party in his various official residences.

On Sunday 21 February 1943 he took Frederica and her attendants in a small party up Table Mountain to attend the annual memorial service on the summit. There was some breakdown of the cableway and so the clergyman who was to hold the service did not appear. Because there was a large gathering, as he informed Margaret, he stepped into the breach and gave an address on the spur of the moment. "I am told it was very acceptable. Anyway I saved the situation, and thereafter my small party, which included the Greek royalties, marched down and we took a lunch behind and in the shadow of a mighty rock, and then descended into the forbidden valley."

This was on the slope of Table Mountain, in the catchment area for part of Cape Town's water supply which was closed to the public. However, Smuts and his party not only intruded in the forbidden area but also took off their clothes and bathed in the forbidden waters. However, in his letter to Margaret, he explained that the men and the women bathed in separate pools with the police sentries protecting him on the outposts. "You know the places in Disa Gorge."

Meanwhile his wife Isie also added to his worries when in January 1943 she suffered an attack of thrombosis. She was confined to Groote Schuur in Cape Town where, according to his letter, she was

69

making good progress and was almost her old self again, took her meals with Smuts and Frederica and joined in all the jollities of life at Groote Schuur while the painter Simon Elves painted portraits of Smuts and Frederica after he had completed "his masterpiece of Isie in all her vivacity and suppressed fire", as Smuts explained.

Although at this time Smuts now and then still discussed religion, or the lack of it in modern life, in his weekly letters to Margaret – and now and then still revealed his inner life – it is apparent that the task of writing *Holism of the Spirit* faded into the background while Frederica moved into the main arena, with Smuts and members of his government even organising a fund for Greek relief after the war.

Meanwhile he complained to Margaret that he might have to go to England again after the parliamentary elections in July 1943, and even to America to see President Roosevelt and then back to Parliament "and so to world without end, amen! It is just all drive, drive, drive! And whither? The tempo of our time is destructive of all silences and the repose of the inner life. I wonder whether the inner life will ever adjust itself to this everlasting preoccupation with the outer world." What he did not say was that this was also the end of his attempt to write *Holism of the Spirit*.

In a final letter to Margaret on 9 November 1945 on the subject, he informed her that he had received a request to have *Holism and Evolution* translated into Spanish but he had refused it as so much of the scientific part was really obsolete. "The advance of physics and biology in the last twenty years has really been phenomenal, and my early chapters read like pre-scientific. I wish I could find time to write my second volume, and let the first become antiquarian as it is practically antiquated. But affairs and politics choke my life and almost choke my soul in these end-of-the-age times," was his final decision on *Holism II*.

CHAPTER SIX

Holism and God

At the end of 1945, when Smuts was 75 years old, he finally gave up his great ambition to write a sequel to *Holism and Evolution*. But it was not the end of his deep interest in religion and in God and matters of the spirit. In fact it is apparent from letters to Margaret during the last five years of his life that religion played an even more important role in his thinking and general philosophic and scientific contemplations.

The mood in these letters, especially after the futile attempts to conclude the peace treaties after the Second World War, is increasingly one of disillusionment, disappointment, almost despair. But then his faith in God, his reading and quotations from the Bible again appear to quicken and inspire him and finally to awake in him an immense feeling of pity; "the religion of pity", as he called it in his letter of 15 October 1945 to Margaret.

Telling her that at last the summer rains had begun, which had saved the situation in the Transkei after a long and devastating drought, he wrote: "We can rejoice again. The wrath is never too long on us in South Africa. But what a wrath on mankind after the war. Have you ever read of a period in history in which there was such a piled up human agony as today? One turns to the newspapers with a feeling of aversion. The war and its mechanical horrors were bad enough. But this milling around of millions of people in all lands, homeless, foodless, hopeless, rotten with disease and drifting like flotsam before the wrath – it is a picture of misery more than one can bear, even to read of, let alone actually experience or witness.

"It is the religion of pity that we are most in need of today. It is curious that this most primitive of kindly feelings is the one most lacking today.

" 'Have pity on us, O Lord' seems to be the prayer rising from millions of hearts to a pitiless heaven. Man's inhumanity to man, as Robert Burns wrote in his poem 'Man was Made to Mourn', finds more dreadful expression today than in the most barbarous periods of which one reads.

"If this is the vengeance which has gone before, how much greater will be the vengeance which will revenge it. What an era of history the new generation is moving into! To think all this is happening in this age when human sensitiveness has been developed to a maximum, increases the moral and physical suffering to an unbearable limit."

And then his religion, his faith in God and his love of God his father and creator returns: "And yet, and yet – there is so much that is good and godlike in man. God so loved the world that he sent his only Son to redeem it and save it. He would not have done it for a godless robot world of man. There is so much that is divine in us, so near is man to God, that it only increases the pain and the horror of this tragedy beyond all comprehension. One can but bow one's head before this revelation of evil, of the evil in us and in our human arrangements. No devil could have conceived something worse than what is our human handiwork. And yet, God so loved the world!

"That is the enigma, the mystery of both evil and good. No wonder that our forefathers could understand it in terms of both God and the Devil. It is both, and no philosophy can argue away this deep-seated duality in human nature."

All this was written on 15 October 1945. Ten days later another soul-searching and deeply religious letter to Margaret followed, after he had received two letters from her which brought him great comfort.

These letters told of her reading and interpretation of John 3 and 17. This reminded him of how puzzled he was to discover where the saying: 'In the world but not of it' comes from. "Well, it is nowhere put in that short form anywhere in the Bible, but it is taken from two verses in John XVII. The whole prayer of Jesus is for his own who are in the world though they are not of it. The quotation is a condensation of what He said, and how neatly and finely it expresses a great spiritual truth. So the new and higher evolves from the lower, but is also beyond it, and immanence and transcendence meet.

"The new spiritual vision is that of the common family life, but raised to a new higher level. God is the father, men are brothers, and the Holy Spirit is that which unconsciously pervades the family group. It is this realism and appeal to our common human experience which makes the gospel such a powerful force. Our more abstract philosophical or theological formulations don't touch this utter simplicity and appeal."

It took one more letter on this high spiritual level before Smuts revealed his inward soul and his vision of holism of the soul that is whole, of the personality that is completely integrated and which is derived from that inner consciousness of struggle which is always with him and still remains unachieved. "O miserable sinner that I am," was his conclusion.

But then again he regains his faith in God and speculates on "how to mobilise that inner subtle spirit, that Holy Spirit, which lies within all great causes; that is the problem. Jesus could do it, Paul in a large measure did it. In a base, degraded way even Hitler could do it and prove the Pied Piper to lead his people to utter destruction. But few have that supreme gift of genius or personality which works miracles."

He was especially conscious of this lack of a great spiritual leader when he took part in the conference at San Francisco at the end of 1945 to devise a peace structure for the world. On 9 November 1945 he wrote to Margaret that while he was there the passage from John 17:21, "I and my Father are one" kept ringing in his mind. "Is there any other way out of the problems of mankind except this union of the human with the divine? Is the world not saved by the divine at the heart of it, and can our economic scientific society be saved without a deeper religious outlook? Is it the Man of Galilee, or another like him born out of distressful conditions who will point the way out of the darkness in which we are milling around?"

He told Margaret that he himself could not see his way through the social and economic tangle of the world. Somehow it seemed that God was not stretching out his Hand to mankind at present. "Will holism do without the holistic Personality?" was his final question.

It was in this deeply religious mood after the Second World War that Smuts was constantly thinking of men of wide spiritual leadership and appeal who could do missionary work on a worldwide basis like Paul who carried the Gospel of Jesus to the Gentiles. He felt that

73

his holism could be a vehicle to bring this about, but sadly he lacked the time, the vitality and the power to carry this to a successful conclusion.

When he died five years later in 1950, after his own people had rejected him in the general election of 1948 – "they have crucified me, they have crucified me" was his cry of anguish and despair – his vision of a holistic future would have come to an end had it not been for a few scientists who followed in his holistic footsteps without, however, giving him any credit or even recognition as the creator of the concept of holism.

Here I am thinking especially of Professor Paul Davies of the University of Newcastle-upon-Tyne with his brilliant book *God and the New Physics*; Professor David Bohm, Professor of Theoretical Physics at Birkbeck College in London with *Wholeness and the Implicate Order*; Professor Stephen Hawking, the wheelchair-bound cosmologist at Cambridge University, author of the best-selling *A Brief History of Time*; Nobel laureate Erwin Schrödinger with *What is Life?*, which is already regarded as one of the great classics of this century; as well as other exponents of the quantum theory which has revolutionised physical science ever since Max Planck in 1900 introduced microelectronics to the world, side by side with Einstein's relativity theory which brought about nuclear energy and the atomic bomb.

Professor Davies is probably the physicist who best explained the radical reformulation of the most fundamental aspects of reality which have come about this century. He ascribes this to Einstein's and Planck's theories, which seemed to turn common sense on its head and found closer accord with mysticism rather than materialism.

"The fruits of this revolution are only now starting to be plucked by philosophers and theologians," he wrote in 1983 when the book first appeared, then he continued: "Many ordinary people too, searching for a deeper meaning behind their lives, find their beliefs about the world very much in tune with the new physics. The physicist's outlook is even finding sympathy with psychologists and sociologists, especially those who advocate a *holistic* approach to their subjects."

I have taken the liberty of italicising the word "holistic" which Davies used here – the word coined by Smuts.

The contention of physicists that only two momentous theories of reality were proposed by scientists in the first quarter of this century, namely the theory of relativity and the quantum theory is in my view not entirely correct. What about Smuts's theory of holism?

Whereas both Einstein and Planck, as well as Darwin and all other scientists before them, used the analytic or reductionist method of cutting up an organism or taking a problem apart to try to find its essence or to solve a problem, Smuts was the first in modern times to introduce the holistic or synthetic method where the emphasis falls on the organism as a whole, or where the unity of a structure rather than the isolated parts or the cut-up bits, are analysed to try to find the essence or inner structure. What Smuts discovered with his holistic method is that a whole is greater than the sum of its parts.

It is significant that the *Oxford Dictionary of the English language* in accepting holism as a new word in the English language credits Jan Christiaan Smuts with its invention in 1926. This, in my experience, is the first and only official recognition of Smuts as the father, the creator and the originator of the word and the concept.

Why do the scientists withhold this honour from Smuts? It may be true that he was probably more of a philosopher than a true analytical scientist, but so were Plato and Aristotle and also in a way Emmanuel Kant, all honoured as great thinkers in both science and philosophy.

What is also remarkable is that a brilliant scientist, as Professor Davies eminently is, even in the preface of his book introduces the "holistic approach" and thereafter in the main body *God and the New Physics* constantly uses the word "holistic" to describe nature, life and mind. He even pleads for additional holistic laws for the holistic features of a physical system, holistic laws that cannot be reduced to the fundamental laws of elementary forces and particles.

I will say more about this in a fuller discussion of how his acceptance of holism in the new physics corresponded to the second book on holism of the spirit which Smuts intended to write. Had Smuts been alive in 1985 when Davies's book *God and the New Physics* first appeared he would undoubtedly have hailed it as the great breakthrough in the concept of holism which he was always expecting during his lifetime. Often in his letters he refers to this: When will they (the scientists) ever accept holism or take it seriously?

Let me meanwhile introduce the other scientists of the new physics who also accept aspects of Smuts's holism or his emphasis

75

on the whole and wholeness in science and philosophy. I have already referred to Professor David Bohm's book *Wholeness and the Implicate Order* which in my view gives a brilliant explanation of the quantum theory and proposes a new model of reality based on wholeness with the notion of the implicate order in which any element contains, enfolded within itself, the totality of the universe, both in regard to matter and consciousness.

Like Smuts, Bohm combines both science and philosophy and also like Smuts fully accepts the whole and wholeness in nature, life and mind as the basis of all reality. On page 17 of his book he even twice used Smuts's creation "holistic" but immediately tells why he rejects "some kind of integrating or unifying 'holistic' principle on our self-world view, for any form of fixed self-world view implies that we are no longer treating our theories as insights or ways of looking but rather as 'absolutely true knowledge of things as they really are'. So, whether we like it or not, the distinctions that are inevitably present in every theory, even an 'holistic' one, will be falsely treated as divisions, implying separate existence of the terms that are distinguished."

This is beyond me, but I find it interesting that Bohm later in his book came to the conclusion that both the quantum theory as well as Einstein's relativity, although very different from one another, "yet in some deeper sense they have in common this implication of undivided wholeness".

It undoubtedly would have pleased Smuts a great deal to think that his holism also forms the basis of both of the great physical theories of this century.

As I have already pointed out, Bohm, although rejecting the word "holistic", later in his book coined his own definition of a hologram, derived from the Greek words *holos* meaning "whole", and *gram,* meaning "to write", as "an instrument that can help give a certain immediate perceptual insight into what can be meant by undivided wholeness".

Unlike Smuts and Davies he does not deal with spiritual issues, but in discussing consciousness and the implicate order he referred to the famous French philosopher Descartes who described matter as "extended substance" and consciousness as "thinking substance". He sees this as basically similar to his own division of reality into explicate and implicate order.

He is of the opinion that "in a certain sense Descartes was perhaps anticipating that consciousness has to be understood in terms of an order that is closer to the implicate than to the explicate. However, when we start, as Descartes did, with extension and separation in space as primary for matter, then we see nothing in this notion that can serve as a relationship between matter and consciousness, whose orders are so different.

"Descartes clearly understood this difficulty and indeed proposed to resolve it by means of the idea that such a relationship is made possible by God, who being outside of and beyond matter and consciousness (both of which He indeed created) is able to give the latter 'clear and distinct notions' that are currently applicable to the former."

Bohm reported that "since then the idea that God takes care of this requirement has generally been abandoned, but it has not commonly been noticed that thereby the possibility of comprehending the relationship between matter and consciousness has collapsed".

Unfortunately, Bohm, in his discussion of the enfolding-unfolding universe and consciousness, was not able to restore this happy God-inspired relationship between matter and consciousness, although he does propose a further survey of the totality of existence "as a whole", which would have pleased Smuts.

Our next member of the community of the new scientists, although in a wheelchair, is much more successful in combining God and the modern science. Paralysed by a degenerative neuromuscular disease, Professor Stephen Hawking, who at the time of writing is the Lucasian Professor of Mathematics at Cambridge University, holds the post once held by Sir Isaac Newton and later by Paul Dirac, two celebrated scientists of the very large and the very small. Hawking speaks to people by means of a speech synthesizer, while a small personal computer is also mounted on his wheelchair.

With these mechanical aids he has done research and in 1988 produced *A Brief History of Time* which is regarded as the scientific best seller of all time. It is a book about time but also about God who fills the pages as Hawking embarks on a quest to answer Einstein's famous question about whether God had any choice in creating our universe. In order to answer this riddle, Hawking, as he explicitly states, is trying to understand the mind of God.

He is to my mind by far the best and the clearest exponent of the quantum physics of Planck and the uncertainty principle of Heisenberg, which were combined in the new theory of quantum mechanics. This governs the behaviour of transistors and integrated circuits, as essential components of modern electronic devices such as television sets and computers, and also forms the basis of modern chemistry and biology.

These inventions have led to new technologies which have created radar, X-rays, microwaves, television, semi-conductors and lasers, and have added a vast amount of new information to the storehouse of human knowledge.

Unbeknown to Smuts in the 1920s when he wrote the final version of *Holism and Evolution*, three fairly unknown scientists at the time, Werner Heisenberg, Erwen Schrödinger, whom I have already mentioned, and Paul Dirac formulated the quantum concept and existing mechanics into a new theory called quantum mechanics, based on the uncertainty principle. As Hawking explains, in this theory particles no longer have separate well-defined positions and velocities that can be observed. Instead they have a quantum state, which is a combination of position and velocity.

As is now generally known, quantum mechanics does not predict a single definite result for an observation. It predicts instead a number of possible outcomes and tells us how likely each of these is. On this basis one cannot predict the specific result of an individual measurement or observation, but different results. This means that quantum mechanics introduces the unavoidable element of unpredictability or randomness into science.

The joke in scientific circles is that Einstein objected very strongly to this aspect of modern science in spite of the important contribution he made in the development of relativity and other aspects of the new physics. As is well known, he was even awarded a Nobel Prize for his contribution to the quantum theory. But it is also well known that Einstein never accepted that our universe was governed by chance. His famous retort to this theory was his statement: "God never plays dice."

Like Smuts's holism, it took many years before quantum mechanics was accepted, but once scientists realised that the experiments were successful, it spread rapidly and is now, more than 70 years since its inception, regarded as the most outstandingly successful scientific theory which has revolutionised both science and technology.

Time magazine in April 1990 calculated that these breakthroughs in physics, due to quantum mechanics which created whole new industries and technologies, now produce as much as a quarter of the US gross national product. All this stems from the discoveries in quantum physics made between 1910 and 1930 on the basis of Planck's original discovery of 1900.

Unfortunately the same cannot be said for Smuts's holism which stems from the same period in human development. It was of course not meant as a technological or mechanical breakthrough, but mainly as a philosophical explanation of the wholeness of the universe: all reality including matter, life and mind as well as the God-given spirit of man. In stressing the importance of the whole and the wholeness of life and all reality Smuts opened a new door to both science and philosophy. This coincided with the new understanding of space and time which was to revolutionise our view of the universe. As Hawking explains, the old idea of an essentially unchanging universe that could have existed, and could continue to exist forever, was replaced by the notion of a dynamic, expanding universe that seemed to have begun a finite time ago, and that might end at a finite time in the future.

Although Hawking started off mainly studying black holes, since 1981 his interest has focused on questions about the origin and fate of the universe which, according to all the observational evidence started off very hot and cooled as it expanded. On this basis he drew up a list of questions about the early universe: Why was it so hot, why is the universe so uniform on a large scale? Why is it still expanding? Was there a big bang and a space-time boundary?

He writes that science seems to have uncovered a set of laws that, within the limits of the uncertainty principle, tell us how the universe will develop with time, if we know its state at any one time. According to him these laws might have originally been decreed by God, who might have chosen the initial configuration of the universe for reasons that we cannot hope to understand.

"It would be very difficult to explain why the universe should have begun in just this way, except as an act of God who intended to create beings like us," is his contention.

However, he reminds his readers that with the advent of quantum mechanics we have come to recognise that events cannot be predicted with complete accuracy, but that there is always a degree of uncertainty. "If one likes, one could ascribe this randomness to the intervention of God, but it would be a strange kind of intervention; there is no evidence that it is directed to any purpose. Indeed, if it were, it would by definition not be random (or uncertain)."

To solve these fundamental problems of the universe and the origin of life and mind and intelligence Hawking looks forward to scientists eventually producing a complete, consistent, unified theory as a first step towards our final goal of a complete understanding of the events around us and of our own existence. He regrets the fact that modern philosophers have not been able to keep up with the advance of the new scientific theories, and have therefore not been able to give answers to the question why the universe was created.

He pleads for a concerted effort on the part of philosophers, scientists and just ordinary people to discover a complete answer to the question why it is that we and the universe exist. "If we find the answer to that, it would be the ultimate triumph of human reason – for then we would know the mind of God", is his final conclusion.

Although in *A Brief History of Time* Hawking never refers to Smuts and his holistic theory, the spirit in which the book was written, as well as the subject matter, correspond very much with Smuts's religious views and his concept of the wholeness of life and all existence as a gift of God.

Smuts would also have been deeply interested in the book of another of the new physicists, Erwin Schrödinger, an Austrian scientist who in 1927 became Max Planck's successor at the University of Berlin after he had discovered wave mechanics during his stay in Arosa in 1925. For this brilliant scientific achievement he was awarded the Nobel Prize for Physics.

In the spring of 1933 he was offered by F. A. Lindermann, who later became Lord Cherwell, a fellowship at Magdalen College in Oxford. It was also at this time that I came to Oxford as a Rhodes Scholar from South Africa, and heard of this brilliant scientist with his invention of wave mechanics which contributed to the quantum theory. The great revelation of this theory, according to him, was that features of discreteness had been discovered in the book of nature, in a context in which everything other than continuity seemed to be absurd according to the views held until then.

When I left Oxford in 1936, by a strange coincidence Schrödinger also left Oxford. He was offered a chair at Edinburgh University in Scotland and another at Graz in Austria. He chose the latter, which he later admitted was a very foolish decision, as he was undermined by the Nazis and had to flee in 1938 to Dublin in Ireland to avoid Nazi persecution.

He wrote two books: *What is Life?*, dealing with the physical aspect of the living cell, and *Mind and Matter* as well as some autobiographical sketches. These were all combined in 1958 into one book: *What is Life?* and published by the Cambridge University Press.

Although a renowned scientist, one of the most brilliant of the new physicists, Schrödinger was also deeply religious like Smuts, and devoted one chapter in his book to science and religion, while he also gives a penetrating analysis of ethics. He gives prominence to Spinoza's well-known explanation that every particular thing or being is a modification of the infinite substance, that is of God. It expresses itself by each of its tributaries, firstly by its bodily existence in space and time, and secondly in the case of a living man or animal by his mind. But he also accepts Spinoza's view that any inanimate bodily thing is at the same time also "a thought of God".

Schrödinger, like Smuts, goes back to Greek civilisation two thousand years before to show that even then the Greek philosophers held the same view. "After Spinoza, the scientist Gustav Fechner, did not shy at even attributing a soul to a plant, to the earth as a celestial body and to the planetary system. I do not fall in with these fantasies, yet I should not like to have to pass judgement as to who has come nearer to the deepest truth, Fechner or the bankrupts of rationalism," was his summing up, with which Smuts would probably have agreed. For Schrödinger, "when God is experienced, this is an event as real as an immediate sense perception or as one's own personality". This is in line with Smuts's own views and experience.

Important and interesting as these revelations of the new physicists are in relation to Smuts's own views, even though they do not all refer to his holism, the most holistically outspoken of them is undoubtedly Paul Davies in his book *God and the New Physics*. I have already mentioned that Smuts, had he been alive when this book appeared in 1983, would have hailed it as the final acceptance of his theory of holism by the scientific community, something for which he had waited until his dying day in 1950. To my mind and based on my research into his plans for a follow-up to *Holism and Evolution*, Davies's book *God and the New Physics* represents in many ways *Holism II*, or *Holism of the Spirit* which Smuts intended to write.

What is remarkable is that Davies, without once mentioning Smuts's name or giving him any credit, completely identifies with the central idea of Smuts's holism that "the whole is greater than the sum of its parts". He also fully accepts Smuts's distinction in analysing an object or a problem as holism versus reductionism. Holism retains the object or the problem as a whole, thereby not altering it or destroying it in the process of analysis, while reductionism, in reducing or taking the object or problem apart in the act of analysing it, destroys its essence.

Like Smuts, Davies explains that the main thrust of Western scientific thinking over the last three centuries had been reductionist. "Indeed the use of the word 'analysis' in the broadest context nicely illustrates the scientist's almost unquestioning habit of taking a problem apart to solve it. But of course some problems (such as jigsaws) are only solved by putting them together – they are synthetic or holistic in nature. The picture on a jigsaw, like the speckled newspaper image of a face, can only be perceived at a higher level of structure than the individual pieces – the whole is greater than the sum of its parts."

Davies also quotes other writers like Arthur Koestler and Donald MacKay, who are well-known defenders of Christian doctrine as supporters of the holistic outlook. Their purpose is to retain values and the higher meaning and purpose of life and all living creatures by stressing the whole and not meaningless isolated pieces. "We may say that the message is on a higher level of structure than circuits and lamps: it is a holistic feature," is his explanation.

Smuts as a devout Christian who valued all life and nature and reality as the creation of God, would have been delighted by this outlook of Paul Davies, Arthur Koestler, Donald MacKay and others who have been quoted. But he would also have been thrilled that at last in a serious scientific treatise his concept of holism and his holistic view of life had been so fully and readily accepted.

Davies's book bristles with the word "holistic": life is a holistic phenomenon; there is the holistic nature of life; there is a holistic view of the act of measurement; a holistic description of two points of view; the holistic discussion of mind and body; the mind is holistic; the soul is a holistic concept; time asymmetry, like life, is a holistic concept; many observed phenomena are of a collective or holistic character; there is a strong holistic flavour to the quantum aspects of nature; God is the supreme holistic concept. Right up to the final paragraph of the book the word "holistic" contributes towards an understanding of the world in all its aspects.

Surely Smuts, the originator of holism, would have welcomed Davies's fascinating book and his extensive acceptance and use of the holistic concept to describe the beauty and mystery of life in our precious universe. At last one scientist has taken holism seriously.

But it is not only this extensive use of his holism which would have pleased Smuts, but in addition the fact that Davies is also deeply religious and gives a brilliant scientific justification of religion and the existence of God. He points out that the brain is the medium of expression of the human mind.

"Similarly the entire physical universe would be the medium of expression of the mind of a natural God. In this context God is the supreme holistic concept, perhaps many levels of description above that of the human mind."

Davies goes even further. He writes that in accepting that life is a holistic concept and that similarly the mind is also a holistic concept, the modern Christian doctrine has moved a long way towards the picture of the whole man through Christ, rather than the traditional idea of a distinct immortal soul being cast adrift from its material counterpart to carry on a disembodied existence somewhere.

This is in line with Smuts's view that the risen Christ is a real personality, a whole man and not merely an immortal soul or a ghostlike figure floating around or adrift from its material existence. Christ retains his wholeness in the combination of body, soul, mind and faith as the Son of God. As such, after his crucifixion He was seen as a whole man first by Mary, afterwards by the apostles and subsequently by Paul and others, and even today the Risen Christ forms the basis of the change and conversion in the lives of innumerable people in many lands.

It would also have pleased Smuts that Davies in explaining the quantum theory as primarily a practical branch of physics also introduced holism in regard to a single totality of the world as part of his explanation. Stating that the quantum theory demolishes some cherished common sense concepts about the nature of reality, it introduces a strongly holistic element in our world view by blurring the distinction between subject and object.

In dealing with the subject of time he states that it is a mistake to overlook "the fact that time asymmetry, like life, is a holistic concept, and cannot be reduced to the properties of individual molecules". He also finds that there is a strongly holistic flavour to the quantum aspects of the nature of matter, interlocking levels of description with everything somehow made up of everything else and yet still displaying a hierarchy of structure: "It is within this all-embracing wholeness that physicists pursue the quest for the ultimate constituents of matter and the ultimate, unified force."

What is even more important is that he found evidence for an element of "cosmic design" that nature has assigned to her fundamental constants while "the delicate fine-tuning in the values of the constants, necessary so that the various branches of physics can dovetail so felicitously, might be attributed to God". However, Davies also warns that it would be foolish, in spite of the spectacular successes of modern science, to suppose that the fundamental questions concerning the existence of God, the purpose of the universe, or the role of mankind in the natural or supernatural scheme have been answered by these advances. "Indeed, scientists themselves have a wide range of religious beliefs."

Finally, claiming that science offers a surer path than religion in the search for God, Davies expresses his deep conviction that it is only by "understanding the world in all its many aspects – reductionist and holist, mathematical and poetical, through forces, fields and particles as well as through good and evil – that we will come to understand ourselves and the meaning behind the universe, our home".

Smuts, especially during the last three years of his life, was also conscious of this and expressed the hope that his holism would supply this understanding of our universe and especially of the human personality, which he regarded as the highest point of development. In a letter to Margaret on 6 February 1946 he refers to a review of Bertrand Russell's *History of Philosophy*, calling it a searching and valuable review which coincides with his own view.

"The insoluble problem for Russell in his philosophy is to account for personality which I consider basic to philosophy and indeed for all knowledge of values.

"Russell's doctrine is really much like Hume's – he also analyses experience into its ultimate elements, but fails to show how from these elements (sense data and sensibilia) you can get to the whole (personality) of which they constitute the elements . . . Holism is the clue – exclude that, and you are left with titbits of experience which you cannot reverence or worship or indeed think of any value at all. Why will people not take holism seriously?"

This question was asked in 1947, 36 years before the appearance of *God and the New Physics*. Smuts here again stressed his belief in the Holy Spirit. "At bottom we are more spiritual than physical in our nature – the inmost core of our being is spirit and not body."

In April 1948 an American scientific expedition was sent to South Africa to enquire into prehistoric life and palaeontology. Professor Camp from Berkeley University and his wife were the leaders of the expedition and called on Smuts. In a letter to Lady Daphne Moore on 8 April 1948 he wrote about their discussions: "We discussed the rise of man through the hundreds of thousands of years, of which there is abundant evidence in South Africa. We discussed holism and its part in evolution.

"Why is it that there is an upward trend in evolution, and higher and more advanced forms arise from lower, more primitive forms? Why is there a curiously pronounced progress towards the higher? Is there direction, is there a trend, a bias in that direction? Is there design and Providence?

"That of course is the central problem in the great mystery of life. Matter runs down like water, life and mind rise up to ever higher levels. How and why is this? I tried to explain how my theory of holism tries to account for this tendency, which is so apparent and yet so mysterious, on purely scientific lines of thought. I hope I did not confuse them.

"I told them I intended still to continue my work on holism and deal with some of the deeper problems which I deliberately left alone in my earlier work. The question is just whether I can live and remain sane enough to do this! The indications are that my party shall win the elections once more, and that I shall be compelled to 'carry on as prime minister. But how long, O Lord.' Will there be no quiet after-

85

noon for release and reflection? The burden and the strain continues."

Here Smuts was terribly mistaken in predicting that he and his United Party would win the general election on 28 May 1948. I was the editor in chief of five of his Afrikaans newspapers at the time, and through my contacts with the public it was clear to me that there was a great deal of dissatisfaction with his government, and that the more conservative sections also objected to his romantic relationship with Princess Frederica of Greece and other women friends, as I have discussed in *The Romantic Smuts*. I regarded it as my duty to inform him of this. He listened patiently but dismissed me and my news as irrelevant. But when the election took place and he was beaten by a boyhood acquaintance, Dr D. F. Malan, and his National Party, Smuts was deeply hurt and upset, and saw himself as a second Jesus in stating: "They have crucified me, they have crucified me", as I have already mentioned.

This electoral defeat was the first devastating blow in his 78th year. More were soon to follow. In October 1948 his eldest son Japie died suddenly of acute cerebral meningitis. As was his custom he was quick to tell Margaret about it. The letter dated 11 October 1948 explains: "This date 11 October is a mark of calamity in my history. On it fifty years ago the Boer War was declared. On it at 12.30 this morning Japie passed away after an illness of less than twenty-four hours. 'Death the most holy' had once more come into this family after a long, long absence and taken away perhaps the pick of the bunch, rather snatched him away without notice . . . what more can one say?

"It is curious that last week I had been reading two philosophical discussions on immortality – one by Professor A. D. Ritchie and another by A. N. Whitehead. Both very high-class and highbrow, but missing the human poignancy of it all. To me the last word in all great matters is 'mystery'. And death, the most natural of all events is also the most mysterious – beyond all philosophy, and perhaps beyond all religion. 'O death, where is thy sting?' But the sting is in those who remain behind, and no consolation of philosophy or comfort of religion has drawn that sting, in spite of the wonderful words of St Paul on the matter.

"In days like these and on an occasion in my life like this, I sense the Eternal within all this transitory scene. It is not all ugliness and misery and pain. The tragedy is highlighted with gleams of the ultimate Good and Beautiful and True – with Faith, Hope and Charity too."

As if this great blow of Japie's sudden death after the disaster of the general election were not enough, in December 1948 two further blows struck Smuts and South Africa in the sudden loss within days of two of Smuts's most brilliant key supporters, Dr Hendrik van der Byl, South Africa's greatest industrialist, and Jannie Hofmeyr, South Africa's most distinguished parliamentarian, whom Smuts had regarded as his successor as leader of his party and as the brilliant intellectual who would solve South Africa's racial problems as he had solved her financial problems during the Second World War.

These four shocks of 1948 dominated his outlook as he entered the last two years of his long, active life. A lesser personality would have been totally destroyed by the combination of defeat and personal and national tragedies. Somehow Smuts not only survived, but was able to assure his friends that he was able to carry on. In a letter to Margaret on 22 March 1949 he asked her not to be unduly concerned about him, or his election or other troubles. "I can take things philosophically and 'can take it' as they say.

"I have a curious inner faith, which I suppose is a sort of laziness or indifference, but yet is restful and prevents one from being worn down by vain endeavour. It is a spirit of acceptance, when I have nothing particular to blame myself for. There is a contrariety in things, a general refractory character in the universe and in life which we must accept, or otherwise go under in friction and frustration. I believe faith has something to do with it – a vague sense of holding on in spite of it all. It certainly keeps me going."

And then in 1950, Smuts and the whole of South Africa were looking forward to the celebration of his 80th birthday. The year started badly for him when he had to fly in an old-fashioned plane from Pretoria to Cape Town and the journey took four long hours. He wrote to "Mama", his wife, that he had to sit the whole day on his bottom and the pain in his back and left hip became more and more unbearable. It had started suddenly on his farm Doornkloof shortly before he left for the parliamentary session in Cape Town.

Doctors in Cape Town examined him and found a displaced vertebra and an antitoxin was injected into his back, but it brought no relief and sitting and walking remained very painful. Meanwhile he realised that he had to prepare not only for his 80th birthday, but also for his 53rd wedding anniversary and a journey by air to London in June.

He could not remember the actual date of his wedding and wrote to "Dearest Mama" on 29 April to ask whether "it was today, 29 April or tomorrow 30 April". It was 30 April, but he could not go to Pretoria for the occasion and remained in Cape Town, informing "Mama" that he was not only very busy with parliamentary work, but also with all the preparations for his birthday celebrations on 24 May, after which on Friday 2 June he had to fly to London.

I saw Smuts in April 1950 to discuss preparations for his birthday celebrations in Cape Town and elsewhere. In the course of our discussions, I asked him whether he expected a long life. His answer was that if he could survive the celebrations for his 80th birthday he would enjoy a long life, but the problem was to please everyone and get past his 80th birthday.

These words were prophetic. His daughter, Louis McIldowie, who was a medical doctor and devoted herself to missionary work, described his last days in a letter to one of his woman friends, Florence Lamont, wife of the American banker Thomas Stilwell Lamont. She herself was a Corliss and a well-known political philosopher and one of Smuts's favourite lady friends, as I pointed out in *The Romantic Smuts*.

The Lamonts, who often visited the Smuts family in South Africa, had at one time taken Smuts and his wife and also Louis on a trip to the Victoria Falls in Rhodesia (now Zimbabwe). In her letter to "My dear Aunt Florence", Louis told her how the day before Smuts died "he still sat chatting to us about that glorious trip we did to the Victoria Falls with you and Uncle Tom and said that he must dictate a letter to you to one of us. But alas it was never done."

Louis in her letter also told her how just before his birthday on 24th May 1950 Smuts complained of a pain in his chest suggestive of a coronary thrombosis. "How he got through all his celebrations in various towns I don't know for he was very ill all the time, but would not give in. Two days before he was to leave for England he had a very bad collapse and all his plans were cancelled. For the next six weeks he was extremely ill and several times I called the family in as I thought the end had come.

"Then he improved up to a point and we were all hopeful. A mild bout of flu laid him low again and then it was obvious that his heart was so badly affected that he would never be well again. The last weeks were spent taking him for drives to see the country he loved so much and letting the grandchildren play where he could watch them. My little son – born early in August – gave him great joy and he loved to sit with the little chap sitting on his lap. He died very peacefully and looked so happy in death, with just a suggestion of a smile on his face."

He died on 11 September 1950. Was Smuts in his moment of death thinking of seeing God face to face at last, or did he visualise the personality of the risen Christ on the basis of his holism? We shall never know.

Appropriately, Isie, whom he had so often neglected and hurt with his romantic excursions (as I have related in *The Romantic Smuts*), had the last word. She thanked all those hundreds of friends and well-wishers who had sent letters of condolence to the Smuts family at Doornkloof. One of them was Mrs Bolus of the Cape Town Herbarium. The letter in her fine, beautiful handwriting replied to Mrs Bolus's description of how "the arrival of the Oubaas into the Presence on the other side and the welcome he received there [from God and the angels] amid 'the glorious burst of trumpets' ".

"Ouma", as Isie was generally known and honoured, told Mrs Bolus that that passage was what she liked best in her letter.

The two main tragedies in Smuts's life were that he died before his concept of holism was accepted by the scientists, and that the New South Africa which he had envisaged and planned for after the general election of 1948 only came about forty years after his death. In my final chapter I will reveal what Smuts had in mind for the new nonracial South Africa, and what advice he can still give to F. W. de Klerk and Nelson Mandela in their endeavours to establish the New South Africa for the benefit of all the races and peoples who live in this fair land with its immense potential.

CHAPTER SEVEN

The Christ of Africa: Smuts's vision for South Africa

The high ethical, philosophical and religious principles set out in the previous chapters may be fine, high-minded and inspiring, but how does a politician and world statesman with a reputation for the use of force for the upholding of law and order apply them to the practical problems of politics and statecraft? Surely this is the supreme test where the success or failure of his or her religious beliefs can be determined.

Did Smuts in his practical politics for a multiracial South Africa and in his statecraft as one of the three most important world leaders of the first half of this century do justice to his religion and especially to his acceptance of the person and the teachings of Jesus Christ, or was he a failure as a Christian?

To Smuts the great Liberal leader in Britain, Sir Henry Campbell-Bannerman, showed the way that a true believer should follow in politics and statecraft after the Anglo-Boer War of 1899-1902, when in 1906 he granted self-government to the defeated Boer Republics of Transvaal and the Orange Free State in a supreme gesture of mercy and magnanimity.

Two deeply religious English women, Emily Hobhouse, the angel of mercy to the Boer women and children in the British concentration camps during the Boer War, and Margaret Clark Gillett, deeply rooted in personal religion and guided by the "inner light" of Quaker experience, prepared Campbell-Bannerman for this act of mercy to a gallant foe.

Smuts was in England in 1906, when the British voters put the destiny of England in the hands of the Liberal Party under the leadership of Campbell-Bannerman. Emily and Margaret also paved the way for

Smuts to make contact with Campbell-Bannerman some time later.

What is remarkable is that Smuts in most of his speeches and actions after 1906 always referred to Campbell-Bannerman and the immense influence his greatness of soul had had on him and his policy and actions both in South Africa and later on the world stage.

This was perhaps also the reason why in the last forty years of his life he kept a huge portrait of Campbell-Bannerman behind his desk in his study at Doornkloof. His official biographer, W. K. Hancock, referred to it: "Throughout the past forty years and more he kept alive the memory of the man and in his letters and speeches had often recalled it to others." To Smuts Campbell-Bannerman was "the Rock", a fount of wisdom and magnanimity to guide mankind to a better way of life.

Some readers will probably think it a joke when I say that an article in a school magazine is my main evidence for Smuts's vision and plans for the world and the South Africa he envisaged in the last years of his life. But this is actually the case.

The article under his name appeared in the June 1948 issue of the Glasgow High School Magazine under the heading "Sir Henry Campbell-Bannerman and South Africa."

It was written by Smuts in February 1948, a few months before the general elections of 28 May 1948 which he was confident that he would win. He lost – unfortunately for himself and for South Africa as a whole, because he had planned to start working towards a new dispensation in South Africa after his predicted victory.

In many ways the decision of the white voters to kick out Smuts and his United Party and hand the government of South Africa over to Dr D. F. Malan and his Herenigde National Party was not only the end of Smuts's political career, but ultimately brought about the end of white rule in South Africa 42 years later.

What is not generally known is that even Dr Malan was so sure that Smuts would win the election that he had arranged to undergo a minor operation after the election. When the results in the various constituencies were announced, he listened with a friend on a small radio and was flabbergasted when he realised with each new victory of his party's candidates that he would be the new prime minister.

Early the next morning he was rushed from his seaside home in Hermanus to Cape Town to meet the press and to prepare to take over the government as leader of a party whose main platform in the elections was to introduce apartheid (separation) between the races in South Africa. As a former Dutch Reformed minister and as a cultured human being he was not ready or prepared for this, but as the political leader of a party with a policy of apartheid he was compelled to implement it.

But to return to Smuts and Campbell-Bannerman and the article in the school magazine, where Smuts reveals Campbell-Bannerman's Damascus Road, the event in his life which in trust and magnanimity, and in greatness of soul, brought about a turning point not only in his own life but in the history of South Africa and Britain.

To Smuts this was how Christian love could be practically applied to the politics and statecraft of the world. Although Smuts, as Kenneth Ingham states in his biography *Jan Christian Smuts: The Conscience of a South African*, "in his inner heart . . . could not reconcile himself to the idea of African equality with Whites", he often told me before the election of 1948 that what was vitally necessary was first to educate the black voters before full democracy and equality could be given them, otherwise chaos would result.

Alas, this was not done either by himself or by the other white leaders who came after him but fortunately a worthy Afrikaner leader President F.W. de Klerk, in the year 1990, forty years after Smuts's death, abolished the apartheid policy with the help of Nelson Mandela, who like Mahatma Gandhi before him, was released from prison, Gandhi in India by the British and Mandela by an Afrikaner here in South Africa.

Smuts's article on Campbell-Bannerman, "which I have written with real pleasure and a debt of honour to the memory of a great statesman", as he wrote in a letter to the Glasgow High School, contained some of his recollections on Campbell-Bannerman's share in the granting of self-government to the defeated Boer Republics in the Transvaal and the Orange Free State.

The article is so important as an understanding and a revelation of Smuts's character, policy and action throughout his entire life and also in revealing his vision for South Africa that I wish to quote it here in full. Smuts himself realised how important it was and instructed the editor of the Glasgow School Magazine in a letter of 16 February 1948 not to raise any objections if other papers desired to quote from it or reproduce it as he was sure that the article might attract wider attention.

Undoubtedly Smuts's greatest blunder was his deviation from Campbell-Bannerman's principle of mercy and forgiveness when in 1916 he had the rebel leader Jopie Fourie shot after he was found guilty by a special court because he had gone over to the rebels in his officer's uniform and with his men inflicted heavy casualties on government troops. Surely here was a case for forgiveness in the true Christian spirit, but Smuts could not see his way open to show mercy and Jopie Fourie was shot. He must have regretted his decision for the rest of his life, as he was haunted until his dying day by threats and recriminations and by the memory of Jopie Fourie who became enshrined as a martyr of Afrikanerdom.

Smuts made a second big mistake during the mining strike in 1921-22 when he used extreme force to quell the strike, resulting in many deaths. This shocked his nonviolent Quaker friends and especially Alice Clark, Margaret's sister, who broke off all relations with him and stopped writing to him. It was the end of their friendship.

Did Smuts in this case sin against his Christian religion or was he justified in using force to save the wealth of the Witwatersrand and to set an example to other rebels and strikers? Let us examine the article he wrote on Campbell-Bannerman in 1948 to try to find the answer.

The article begins by stating that the action of Campbell-Bannerman in granting self-government to the Transvaal and the Orange Free State in 1906 would ever remain one of the highlights of British statesmanship, with far-reaching effects on the future course of events.

"In these days of swiftly moving events and fading memories it is right that his great action should be remembered. And the pages of a Magazine conducted by his old Scots school is a proper place in which to record his action once more.

"After the conclusion of the South African War in 1902 crown colony rule of the standard type was imposed on the conquered republics. It was to be feared, in view of the length and obstinacy of the Boer resistance, that there might be a renewal of the trouble. But nothing happened. The behaviour of the Boer people, intent only on rebuilding their homes and restoring their destroyed country, was in every way exemplary. Nothing happened to disturb the peace or internal security. It soon became evident to the British authorities that in a

93

country like the Transvaal, with a Boer population traditionally wedded to law and order, and a British population always restive under the restraint of crown colony rule, the position was becoming untenable. And so in 1905 a plan was evolved by the then Conservative government to grant what is called representative government to the Transvaal; that is to say there would be popular representation in a legislative assembly, but the government would remain under the crown. Both among the Boer and the British inhabitants there was considerable feeling against such a half-way solution, and it was clear to the Boer leaders that the scheme was likely to lead to differences between the British governing authority and the people, and so likely to disturb the good relationship which had existed since the peace.

"Towards the end of 1906 a general election was pending in Britain, and it appeared likely that the Conservative Party might be beaten by the Liberal Party led by Sir Henry Campbell-Bannerman. Personal exchanges between Lord Kitchener and myself at the Peace Conference in 1902 had raised hopes that the Boer people might look forward to a change of the crown colony regime when such a change of government should take place. My colleagues therefore asked me to go to London and explore the position with the new Liberal Government. So I arrived in December 1905 on my errand in London, where I had last been as a student ten years before. My presence was noted, and I remember an evening paper in London making a remark that the most dangerous man then walking the streets was a Boer emissary bent on upsetting the Boer War settlement. This looks a bad prophecy in the light of after events; but it still remains a question whether it might not have been a good shot if my mission had turned out a failure. Little more than ten years later I was once more walking the streets of London, but this time as a member of the British war cabinet, helping in the conduct of the Great War.

"What an extraordinary turn of events which completely upset the newspaper prophecy and amazed the world! The man who wrought the miracle was Sir Henry Campbell-Bannerman, to all appearances an ordinary man, almost commonplace to the superficial view, but a real man, shrewd and worldly wise, but rooted in a great faith which inspired a great action.

"I discussed my mission with many members of the Cabinet – perhaps the most brilliant government Britain had had for a long time, and with men among them like Asquith, Edward Grey, Lloyd George, John Morley, and last but not least Winston Churchill. Campbell-Bannerman looked the least distinguished in that galaxy of talent. But what a wise man, what statesmanship in insight and faith, and what sure grip on the future! My mission failed with the rest, as it was humanly speaking bound to fail. What an audacious, what an unprecedented request mine was – practically for the restoration of the country to the Boers five years after they had been beaten to the ground in one of the hardest and most lengthy struggles in British warfare.

"But with Campbell-Bannerman my mission did not fail. I put a simple case before him that night in 10 Downing Street. It was in substance: 'Do you want friends or enemies? You can have the Boers for friends, and they have proved what quality their friendship may mean. I pledge the friendship of my colleagues and myself if you wish it. You can choose to make them enemies, and possibly have another Ireland on your hands. If you do believe in liberty, it is also their faith and religion.' I used no set arguments, but simply spoke to him as man to man, and appealed only to the human aspect which I felt would weigh deeply with him. He was a cautious Scot, and said nothing to me, but yet I left that room that night a happy man. My intuition told me that the thing had been done.

"The rest of the story has been told by Mr Lloyd George: how at a cabinet meeting next day the prime minister simply put the case for self-government to the Transvaal to his colleagues, and in ten minutes had created such an impression that not a word was said in opposition, and one of the ministers had tears in his eyes.

"A misssion to work out details was sent to the Transvaal, and next year the country had its free constitution, and a government in which the Boer and the Englishman sat together, under a prime minister who had been the commander-in-chief of the Boer armies in the field. But Louis Botha was a man of like stature to Campbell-Bannerman. Greatness of soul met equal greatness of soul, and a page was added to the story of human statesmanship of unfading glory and inspiration to after ages.

"Seven years later Campbell-Bannerman had passed away, but Botha was once more a commander-in-chief in the field, but this time in common cause with Britain and over forces in which both Afrikaners and British were comrades. The contagion of magnanimity had spread from the leaders to their peoples.

"Nor does the story end there. It was continued in the Second World War, after Botha had also passed away. It has even been suggested that the action of South Africa saved our cause in the years that followed the Battle of Britain and when America had not entered the war. The story may never end. To great deeds wrought by the human soul there is no end.

"Today we are living in distraught times, where in the confusion it is not easy to recognise the way. But in this simple story I have told there is a light of statesmanship which shines like an inextinguishable beacon above the raging storm. We shall remember Campbell-Bannerman.

"Last year, 1947, when the royal family visited South Africa, the King did my simple house (a relic from the British military camp of the Boer War) the honour of a visit. There in my study he saw a large portrait of Campbell-Bannerman hanging above my chair. And later he said to me: 'I was so glad to see that portrait in your study. One seldom sees it in Britain today.' Alas!

"And so I say to my young Scots friends, and my friends in all our Commonwealth, and to mankind everywhere where greatness of soul is honoured: Don't forget Campbell-Bannerman."

This "contagion of magnanimity" based on trust and greatness of soul which Smuts mentioned in the article became the foundation stone of his own statesmanship from 1906 until his death. It also inspired his vision for a South Africa where all the races and peoples could work together and co-operate to build a great, peaceful, prosperous state to take its place in the community of nations in the world.

In the article, Smuts mentioned his personal discussion with Kitchener at the Peace Conference in 1902 which might have played a role in bringing about this great transformation with such tremendous results both in Britain and South Africa, as mentioned in the article. Later, after his death, I learnt of another source which also influenced Campbell-Bannerman.

Emily Hobhouse and her Quaker friends of Street in Somersetshire in England, who supported the Liberal Party, also helped to prepare the way for Smuts when he visited Campbell-Bannerman in 1906.

Through Hobhouse, Smuts got to know the Clarks. The three daughters, Margaret, Alice and Hilda, met and became friendly with Smuts and through him learnt of the deep and sincere religion of the Boers and their faith in God. Campbell-Bannerman, although a devout Presbyterian, also took an interest in the Quaker religion and might have been influenced by the Clarks and Hobhouse to receive and talk to Smuts.

Margaret told me about it when I saw her shortly after Smuts's death in 1950. I have described her recollections in *The Romantic Smuts*.

In 1919, after the early death of Louis Botha, Smuts became prime minister of South Africa and applied the "contagion of magnanimity" which he had learnt from Campbell-Bannerman to the relationship between the British and the Afrikaners. Unfortunately his path of peace and friendship between the two white races was constantly blocked by strikes, the aftereffect of the rebellion of 1914 and by wars and depression. But these setbacks did not deter him. He continued to preach friendship and co-operation between the two groups until his dying day.

During the Second World War, when he regained the leadership of South Africa as an ally of Britain in the struggle against Hitler, he felt that he was at last succeeding in uniting the Afrikaners and the English, especially when he played a prominent role in securing victory.

In 1947 he followed up this success by bringing the British royal family on a lengthy official visit to South Africa, a great feather in his cap.

It was in this period of his life that his thoughts turned to plans to include the so-called native races of South Africa in the democratic process and give them a stake in the future of South Africa. His intention was to tackle this problem, the biggest problem in South Africa, as he called it, after the election of 1948.

With this end in view he started in his discussions and especially in his letters to his friends to clarify his thoughts and to indicate on what basis and under which conditions he was prepared to extend the democratic process to all the inhabitants of South Africa. But as was his custom, and because he regarded himself not only as prime minister of South Africa but as a world leader, his letters and discussions covered a wide area of statecraft, philosophy, science and religion.

One of the most difficult problems which Smuts had to deal with at this time was the future status of the Indian community of more than

300 000 in South Africa, especially as a result of the direct intervention of Mahatma Gandhi who, after his release from prison, was
bestriding British and world politics like a giant. Gandhi kept on
directly interfering in South African affairs, much to the annoyance of
Smuts.

Smuts and Gandhi had first clashed in 1907, shortly after the Transvaal had received self-government from Britain. Gandhi, who arrived
in South Africa in 1894, had meanwhile started his Satyagraha movement based on "soul force", using methods of passive resistance and
nonviolence to force British and South African leaders to give democratic rights to Indians in India and South Africa respectively.

What made this clash between Smuts and Gandhi so important and
yet so strange was that they as personalities were so different but at
the same time so like one another in the deepest essences of their
beings, their interest in religion and their actions and outlook. They
were different from the point of view of their origins in that Gandhi
was born in India, a member of the Eastern civilisation, a Hindu by
race and religion, while Smuts was a Westerner and part of the cultured civilisation of the West and a Christian in his religion.

By a coincidence they were born practically at the same time,
Gandhi in 1869 and Smuts in 1870; both went for their higher educa-
tion to England, Gandhi to London, Smuts to Cambridge; both studied
law; both were deeply religious although with different religious
backgrounds; both were more interested in making contact with God
through contemplation, study, thought, prayer and salvation.

Gandhi was locked up by the British in the Yeravda jail after he had
left South Africa and returned to India at the outbreak of the First
World War. A friend persuaded him to write his autobiography while
in jail. He promptly wrote an extraordinarily brilliant book which
appeared in 1927. Written in Gujarati, it was translated into English in
1940.

His main theme in the book was to describe his striving and pining
to achieve self-realisation, to see God face to face and to attain salvation.

To do this he concentrated on discovering truth through experiment
with nonviolence, celibacy and other principles of conduct believed to
be distinct from truth. "But for me truth is the sovereign principle
which includes numerous other principles.

"The truth is not only truthfulness in word, but truthfulness in thought also, and not only the relative truth of our conception, but the Absolute Truth, the Eternal Principle, that is God. There are innumerable definitions of God because his manifestations are innumerable. They overwhelm me with wonder and awe and for a moment stun me. But I worship God as Truth only. I have not yet found Him, but I am seeking after Him. I am prepared to sacrifice the things dearest to me in my pursuit of this quest." This included even his life, as he wrote later.

In spite of their mutual deep interest in religion and their search for and striving after God, Smuts and Gandhi were often at loggerheads. At first they even refused to see one another. Smuts felt that Gandhi was making a nuisance of himself and on 8 December 1913 he was arrested on Smuts's instruction and sentenced to three months' imprisonment. But when fifty thousand Indians offered themselves for imprisonment with Gandhi, Smuts was forced to release him.

It was just at this time that Emily Hobhouse arrived in South Africa to unveil the monument to the 23 000 Boer women and children who had lost their lives in the British concentration camps during the Boer War. She had previously become friendly with Gandhi and supported him in his agitations to obtain democratic rights for the Indians both in South Africa and in India.

Gandhi must have contacted her, for on 29 December she wrote a passionate letter to Smuts pleading with him to see Gandhi personally. "Not being South African or Indian but in fullest sympathy with both it just struck me, since Gandhi asked me, that I might be of some use, so use me or refuse me or abuse me just as it pleases you dear Oom [she always called Smuts *oom* (uncle)]. I am too old and benumbed to mind throwing myself down as a paving stone and being trodden upon as a result."

The outcome was that Smuts relented, followed Hobhouse's advice and arranged a meeting with Gandhi who as a gesture of goodwill called off the march of his followers.

This brought some temporary relief, but pretty soon Gandhi and the Indians in South Africa were again on the warpath with their demands for more rights. Smuts had a difficult time dealing with Gandhi's demands and tactics. So when Gandhi decided to leave South Africa in July 1914 and return to India, Smuts was greatly relieved. "The saint has left our shores," he wrote to Sir Benjamin Robertson on 21 August 1914, "I sincerely hope forever."

And yet this was not the end of their strange friendship and the common bond between them based on their religion. Both Gandhi and Smuts not only had affection for one another but also great admiration. Smuts realised that Gandhi, while in South Africa, was only trying to improve the status of the Indians, and to improve also the conditions under which they lived and worked, while Gandhi on his part never imputed racial prejudice to Smuts and understood the pressures of South African society on him to safeguard white civilisation.

When Smuts became a member of the British War Cabinet in London in 1916, he was able to guide the British leaders in their dealings with Gandhi who was then in India, locked up in a British jail. When the question of granting commissions to Indians in the British Army was brought up in the War Cabinet Smuts strongly supported the proposal.

He himself later told all about it in a speech to an Indian audience in Durban. When it was pointed out to him in the War Cabinet that if commissions were granted to Indians there might be a possibility that Europeans would be placed under Indians, Smuts replied: "Why not, I would be proud to serve under an Indian officer, if he were able."

Smuts wanted Gandhi to know that he was never against him or Indians as such. He wrote a letter to Gandhi explaining his actions and his outlook: "When I was about the same time as you studying in England, I had no race prejudice against your people. In fact, if we had known each other we should have been friends. Why is it then that now we have become rivals, we have conflicting interests? It is not colour prejudice or race prejudice, though some of our people do ignorantly talk in these terms, but then there is one thing which I want you to recognise. It is this. I may have no racial laws, but how will you solve the difficulty about the fundamental difference of our cultures? Let alone the question of superiority, there is no doubt that your civilisation is different from ours. Ours must not be overwhelmed by yours. That is why we have to go for legislation which must in effect put disabilities on you."

Gandhi understood Smuts's point of view and noted: "If, therefore, we wanted to live in South Africa we must adopt their standard of life, so long as it is not against morality."

Smuts's irritation with Gandhi, but also his admiration for him, increased over the years as Gandhi showed his mettle in India where he single-handedly destroyed the British Colonial system to create both India and Pakistan, after a bloody war, as independent states, but brought about eventual reconciliation between Britain and India. It is on this basis that historians regard the first encounter between Smuts and Gandhi in South Africa as of deep significance, almost as much as the contact between Smuts and Campbell-Bannerman.

When Gandhi's 70th birthday was celebrated worldwide in 1939, Smuts contributed an article on "the principle of suffering", which he thought lay at the root of Gandhi's famous Satyagraha, using "soul force" through passive resistance and nonviolence as his political methods. "It was my fate to be the antagonist of a man for whom even then I had the highest respect," was his summing up of his encounters with Gandhi in South African politics.

Gandhi had previously sent Smuts a pair of sandals which he had made by hand when Smuts had him locked up in a South African prison. Smuts always regarded them as a treasured relic and sent a photograph of the sandals to Gandhi on the occasion of his 70th birthday. As Hancock points out in his book on Smuts, these sandals were still in Smuts's possession when he heard that Gandhi had been assassinated on 30 January 1948 by a Hindu who held him responsible for the partition of India and Pakistan. Smuts's comment was: "A prince of men has passed away and we grieve with India in her irreparable loss."

Privately he wrote to the British politician L.S. Amery: "Gandhi has played a very large part in the world and produced an effect on opinion which has in some respects surpassed that of any other contemporary of ours. And he succeeded. And his success was due not only to his personality but to strange methods, never resorted to by other leaders. Altogether he was a strange human phenomenon."

Four months after Gandhi's assassination in India Smuts was removed from office by the white voters of South Africa. He wrote to Margaret on 22 March 1949: "South Africa is isolating itself from the world opinion in a world situation which is full of danger. And the South Africans are such a good people, sinning not from evil but more from ignorance as the Greeks would have held."

It was at this time that Smuts was secretly approached by Winston

Churchill, leader of the Conservative Party in Britain, under the nom de plume Colonel Warden, to ask his advice on what to do about India. Following the assassination of Gandhi, Britain had released Pandit Nehru from an Indian jail after sixteen years of imprisonment. Fortunately for Britain, Nehru had shown signs of magnanimity and opposition to communism. Churchill was, however, worried that Nehru as the new Indian leader would declare India a republic outside the British Commonwealth. He thought that that might open the door to a possible Soviet invasion of India. He also felt that South Africa should remain in the Commonwealth and not repudiate the crown. He consulted Smuts about his fears and anxieties.

In a letter on 23 May 1949 Smuts under the nom de plume Henry Cooper, told Churchill that under the new Nationalist government in South Africa a campaign to convert the country into a republic was coming and might be in full spate when he was no longer there to combat it. "Although Dr Danie Malan as prime minister was at heart a moderate – as I have indicated – he would not be able to control his republican extremists who were very powerful. The danger was therefore very real and when it happened it would tear South Africa apart."

However, Smuts was not only worried about the future of South Africa, he had deep doubts and anxieties about the world as a whole. In this rapidly changing world, he felt it impossible to peer too deeply into the future.

"I think the world is moving into one of the secular crises of history, and no one will ultimately emerge from it," he wrote to Churchill and continued: "For the sake of the future I am jealous for the coherence and stability of the Commonwealth which together with American war potential, will save mankind from the rocks as nothing else will."

Smuts then put his finger on one of the main evils of the modern world and especially of the evolving Third World with a substantial part of mankind under its control: "The present tendency to concentrate on social security, without earning it by work, may lead to a fresh outburst of dictatorship, which follows chaotic economic conditions. If democracy cannot provide efficient leadership, the road is open for dictatorship, as recent history has shown. And dictatorship at once leads to a struggle for world power."

It was for this reason that, to him, the prospect before mankind was therefore far from bright. Although he and Churchill would not see it, "the transition through which the world was moving might bring strange developments from which, one hoped, our free Western culture should once more emerge, purified and strengthened", he wrote to Churchill.

It was in this mood of anxiety about the future of mankind that he turned again to his religion and his faith in God and the guidelines of Jesus. In a letter to Professor Gilbert Murray of Oxford he referred to the ordinary people, the common man, "who after all is a very good and human fellow, as long as he does not think he is able to run the world and do things he has never been trained for".

In this connection, however, he liked to think of Jesus with his disciples, his "common men", fishermen and the like, who could pass on to the future the message which they themselves could scarcely understand.

"Surely this is one of the miracles of history, and the greatest tribute to the common man! On the purely human level, there is nothing better and more sincere than the ordinary man. But only on that level."

Smuts thought that it was also on that level that the really good work of our age was being done. "I sometimes feel as if in our confused age the real goodness of the world has retired to family life, to those intimate circles of the home where the flame, now burning so dimly in the great world, is kept going. The great world is not a pleasant or good scene today."

What worried him further was that mankind was moving into a "colour" phase of history, with results none could foresee and South Africa should dread most. He referred to his hopes and anxieties in this regard in an address he delivered on 16 December 1949 at the inauguration of the Voortrekker Monument outside Pretoria. The cornerstone had been laid on 16 December 1938, the centenary of the Battle of Blood River at which the Voortrekkers inflicted a heavy defeat on the Zulus under the leadership of Dingane.

In this address, from which I will quote passages, Smuts reveals his deep religious beliefs, his faith in God and in his guidance of the South African people, as well as his vision of a New South Africa in which all the races could co-operate and work and live in peace. The address was delivered in Afrikaans.

"Today we stand on a vantage point from which we can look back upon three centuries of our history and also, in some measure, forward into the shadows of the future. A nation is not a creation of a day but of centuries of the past as well as of the future. Only in this context, in summing up the long years of a people's existence, do we discern the continuous direction and can form a truer conception of the tendency of our history and of our distant destiny.

"Behind us we see, with the deepest thankfulness, the clear evidence of Higher guidance through deadly dangers, of escape through unforseen paths.

"The more one reflects on the genesis of South Africa, the more one comes to realise that there was more than human planning and human leadership. And what a colourful history as well! What young nation can boast a more romantic history, one of more far-reaching interest? Colour, incident, tragedy and comedy, defeat and victory, joy and sorrow – our early history is full of the most gripping interest.

"If only we had the pen of the Greeks, what a literary contribution we should make to our future treasures? There is gold, not only in our earth, but still more in our history. There was so little sign of any pre-conceived plan, so much mystery. It was as if the Voortrekkers were seeing the invisible."

Here Smuts was quoting from the Bible where in Hebrews 11:27 it describes how Moses, after he chose to suffer affliction rather than enjoy the treasures of Egypt, by faith forsook Egypt, not fearing the wrath of the king; for he endured, as seeing Him who is invisible.

The Voortrekkers, like the Israelites in their urgent need, sought a way out of deeply felt grievances and difficulties. That way out was something quite different from what was foreseen or expected, and so a miracle of history had been born, Smuts declared.

He pointed out how the Voortrekkers in their despair decided to trek away in their ox-wagons, to leave the old beloved farms in the Cape, to move over the Orange River into unknown country and seek a new homeland.

"The beginning was so small, but how astonishing was the outcome. Not only the Voortrekkers but also the creative spirit of history was on a journey to an unknown future. We today on this vantage point can see what no Voortrekker ever dreamed of.

"The astonishing results were partly due to the courage, the persistance, the high qualities of soul which here created an outstanding human drama; and partly to the course of circumstances, the incalculable factor in history, in all history."

104

Smuts then referred briefly to two aspects of the Great Trek which particularly concerned the English settlers in South Africa and the "native" population of the interior where the Voortrekkers had settled. He pointed out that there was a large measure of hearty co-operation between the old Afrikaner population and the new, recently arrived English settlers who came to South Africa in 1820 and settled in the eastern districts of the Cape. There was a good relationship between them and combined action in the frontier wars. Even as regards the Great Trek there was strong English sympathy with the trekkers in their strange undertaking. Witness the Bible which was presented to Jacobus Uys by the Settler community of Grahamstown. Piet Retief in his farewell manifesto makes no reproach against his English fellow-citizens, but only against the government. Again, in Natal there was every evidence of good feeling and good relations between the Voortrekkers and the few settlers at Port Natal; they took part in the battles later fought against Dingane and English blood was shed along with Afrikaner blood. There was no sign of national conflict between the whites.

Similarly, Smuts pointed out, even between the Voortrekkers and the black population of the interior there was no particular ill feeling, although the whites suffered bitterly and heavily from raids and cattle-stealing on the eastern frontier. Witness the safe reconnoitring journey of P. L. Uys in September 1834 through the regions inhabited by blacks to Natal and back in 1835. Witness the many Afrikaners who, at loggerheads with the British government, found safe lodgement with the black tribes – the Bezuidenhouts, Trichardts, Van Rensburgs and many others. Witness the large number of black and coloured servants who accompanied the Voortrekkers on the Great Trek and shared with them the sweet and the sour and even death. Witness the good reception which the Voortrekkers received from various black chiefs, such as, among others, Moroka.

Bad feelings appeared only afterwards as a result of the attacks by Moselekatse on the Vaal river and by Dingane in Natal. Moreover, it must be admitted that neither made a distinction between the Voortrekkers and their own black fellow tribesmen whom they exterminated as mercilessly by the hundred thousand.

In this connection Smuts was at pains to point out that the Voortrekkers' struggle was not against the blacks as such, but against the chiefs who, with their Zulu armies, made a desert of the interior of Natal, the Transvaal and the Orange Free State, and in so doing, unwittingly cleared the country for white settlement.

"In this way the Voortrekkers moved into largely open country where they met and took under their protection the remnants of exterminated black tribes. The accusation that the Voortrekkers robbed the blacks of their land, is for the most part unfounded."

He declared that battles like Vegkop, Mosega, Blood River, Makapaanspoort, as well as other similar incidents, were necessary to punish attacks and to make law and order the heritage of the blacks as well. "The Afrikaners did not follow the policy of extermination which, in other countries solved the native question for the newcomers," was Smuts's final verdict in his address.

Already in 1906, as I have mentioned in *The Holistic Smuts*, Smuts expressed his feeling that strong forces were at work in South Africa which would transform the Afrikaner attitude to the black races in a letter to John X. Merriman. He then felt inclined to shift the intolerable burden of solving the problem to the ampler shoulders and stronger brains of the future. As Ingham states: "Smuts had no answer to offer."

During the last years of his life he felt confident that this would eventually come about in South Africa, but he warned that the way into the future and through the world was never without danger, least of all at that time in the great world revolution which was overshadowing the fate of mankind. "More particularly the path of the European community in this African continent will not be one of roses. So let us not be fanatical about our past and, by romanticising it, get on the wrong track; but let us face the future soberly with open eyes and common sense."

In entering the "colour" phase of history to bring about equality to all the races living in South Africa through democracy and racial cooperation, he warned that none could foresee the results, but he was no less sure that the worst like the best never happens. However, he thought that to ensure a successful outcome South Africa should fulfil three vital conditions:

The first condition was that in applying democracy to all in South Africa, the vital importance of leadership to guide the people on the right path should not be neglected. Democracy is in its essence a school for people to learn the hard lesson of self-government. Their

106

mistakes are part of the schooling and must therefore be accepted as inevitable. "South Africa has, however, so often been right at critical moments that one should not mind smaller incidental mistakes too much," he wrote to Daphne Moore on 1 June 1947.

In a second letter a while later he stressed the importance of leadership as part of democracy. "How poor is democracy without leadership. The temptation should be avoided to seek solutions in slogans and catchwords and party formulas."

The second condition to ensure success for a nonracial South Africa was to avoid the emphasis on rights for the individual and to stress the importance of duties alongside the granting of rights. Smuts regarded this as very important and necessary to ensure stability, growth and development.

In a powerful letter to Chung-Shu Lo, the well-known Chinese philosopher who was connected with Unesco and who approached Smuts for suggestions to improve the world body, Smuts stressed the value of duties for the individual next to rights. "I find our modern emphasis on 'rights' somewhat overdone and misleading. It is a modern way of expression, probably owing something to Rousseau and the French Revolution and the American Declaration of Independence.

"It makes people forget that the other and more important side of rights is duty. And indeed the great historic codes of our human advance emphasised duties and not rights. The laws of Hammurabi, the King of Babylonia who lived some time between 2100 and 1800 B.C. and drew up a code of laws bearing his name; the Ten Commandments in the Old Testament; and the highest and noblest code of men, the Sermon on the Mount of Jesus Christ – all are silent on rights, all lay stress on duties."

Smuts continued: "I dare say your Chinese wisdom follows the same line. If the rule to be just and honest and kind and merciful and compassionate etc. were followed, all would be well with our human society and we shall enjoy the life, self-development, self-expression and enjoyment, which is our share in our earthly space. The rights which are now fashionable, are much too individualistic and give no due recognition to that organic human and social unity which the duties of older codes recognise as the real rule and law and pattern of right living."

Referring to a bill of rights, Smuts stated that this would only be of real value if it dealt with practical rules and guidelines of conduct, rather than with high-sounding phrases which have no practical value. The snares of words and slogans and catchwords would have to be avoided as much as possible in what was going to be a code.

The third condition which he thought even more essential for a new South Africa dealt with the preservation of law and order and the maintenance of a strong force to ensure this. One of his last letters to his great friend Margaret, written on 22 April 1950 – a few months before his death – dealt almost entirely with the necessity of force in the modern world to preserve liberty and the other ideals of Western civilisation.

"I have always looked upon Africa as part of Europe in this connection, and the British as the political core of it. But Africa is drifting sadly, and the Commonwealth is uncertain and confused and weakened beyond belief. A united Western Europe, in which Britain and the Commonwealth play a strong hand as the guardian of our fundamental political ideals is so necessary to the new set-up we wish to establish against the menace of force and anarchy.

"At bottom it is a great moral and spiritual issue. But morals and spiritual idealism are in danger unless valiantly backed up by adequate force of its own. In this sense force is necessary for our faith, and must not be decided as evil. May we prove strong enough to hold the fort of liberty and our civilised human faith in the great power struggle now raging in the world," was his hope for the world and for his beloved South Africa and all Africa, "to which I am so deeply wedded in love and duty. My hope is here, South and North. My work is here, my dream in the North. And beyond that stretches eternity," was the summing up of his life and his advice for the future.

In this regard he also referred to the last message of his great hero, Paul Kruger, who called upon his nation to seek in the past what was good and beautiful and build on that for the future. Only on that deeper foundation of the good and the beautiful and on justice which exalts a people, as it is stated in the Bible, can fruitful co-operation and brotherhood between our white peoples be consolidated and the future of our white community be lastingly ensured.

"On the same ethical, rather than political basis, a solution might also be sought of the greatest problem of our Native relations, the most difficult of all and the final test of our Western Christian civilisation."

But Smuts remained optimistic about the future and the eventual success of change in South Africa until his dying day, based on his faith in the guidance of God and his deep love and admiration of Jesus Christ whose Holy Spirit as a link with God, the Father of mankind and our universe, is with us all our lives.

In 1990, more than forty years after Smuts's death, South African President F. W. de Klerk took the bold decision to release the black leader Nelson Mandela from prison as the first step in a policy of reform to grant full democratic rights to the 26 million blacks in South Africa alongside the six million whites who already enjoyed these rights.

This was a step with far-reaching implications and repercussions comparable to the granting of self-government in 1906 to the defeated Boer Republics – a step Smuts probably would have welcomed as on a par with the "contagion of magnanimity" resulting from Campbell-Bannerman's famous act of statesmanship towards the defeated Boer people.

Today, 44 years after his death, Smuts's message of hope and expectation during his active life, based on his deeply felt religion, his acceptance of Jesus Christ as saviour and coupled with his holistic outlook has at last become a reality in his beloved South Africa.

The pity is that he, with his great spirit, his faith and his wisdom, was not there to see its glorious birth in peace and unity to form "a rainbow nation at peace with itself", as South Africa's new leader, Nelson Mandela, described it at his inauguration on 10 May 1994.

Smuts would surely also have agreed with Mandela when he added these historic words: "The time for the healing of the wounds has come. The moment to bridge the chasms that divide us has arrived - the time to build is upon us."

What makes these three South African leaders of the 20th century – Jan Smuts, F. W. de Klerk and Nelson Mandela – so outstanding is that De Klerk and Mandela are – like Smuts was – deeply religious and sincere Christians, and on the basis of their Christian religion they followed the paths of conciliation and co-operation between different races and nations in South Africa, Smuts between the English and Afrikaans sections and De Klerk and Mandela between the whites, Coloureds, Indians and black races.

109

It was the religion, the insight and the genius of De Klerk at the height of his power as State President to have felt the call to bring about a complete transformation in South Africa by consenting to assist in dismantling his own power.

Hence a miracle was born in South African history when the supreme white leader became ready to assist Mandela as the supreme black leader to lead the country if the electorate so desired. And when it happened and De Klerk made his dignified and gracious concession of defeat the entire world rejoiced and hailed him and Mandela as great leaders and examples to many other states with similar problems.

It was at the time when De Klerk released Mandela that my first book on Smuts, *The Holistic Smuts*, appeared, and I sent one of the first copies to President De Klerk, with a note congratulating him on his wise decision to release Nelson Mandela and to start the negotiations for a new democratic South Africa with equal rights for all the inhabitants. A while later I received a personal note of thanks from President De Klerk in which he wrote in Afrikaans:

"Dis mense soos jy wat my ondersteun wat 'n riem onder my hart is."

It is difficult, if not impossible to translate this sentence literally as it is written in idiomatic Afrikaans which goes back to the days of the Voortrekkers with their ox-wagons when a "riem" (a thong) was an essential ingredient of their culture and their daily activities.

There are therefore a number of idioms based on references to "riem" mentioned in the Afrikaans dictionaries. One of the best of these is the one used by President De Klerk in his letter welcoming my support.

Loosely translated, what he said was that the support of people like me was greatly encouraging to him, yet the meaning of the idiom goes deeper than mere support. It touched the inner recesses of his life, it bore up his heart to give him courage and assurance in the knowledge that he was on the right path towards solving one of the most difficult problems facing not only South Africa but mankind in general.

I therefore valued his letter and became convinced that at last the Afrikaner nation has produced a second Smuts, a new leader who is prepared on the basis of inner conviction to follow the path of justice, fair play, trust, righteousness and magnanimity.

Smuts in a way foresaw the new nonracial South Africa when he

110

delivered his last great speech at the unveiling of the Voortrekker Monument. In his speech he also referred to the monumental cross called the Christ of the Andes, on top of the Andes mountains of South America, between Argentina and Chile, set up after long strife between them as a symbol of eternal peace.

He had a vision of a similar cross, the Christ of Africa, as a symbol not only of past strife, of blood and tears, but also of the reconciliation and eternal peace between white and black not only in South Africa, but also in the whole of Africa, based on our vow always to pursue in our race and colour relations the just, the good and the beautiful which form the bases of our Christian religion.

God willing, maybe it will be possible to erect this cross, The Christ of Africa, on Table Mountain at the foot of Africa, or on a peak of the Drakensberg between Natal and the Orange Free State, or on some mountain peak in the Transvaal, to express Smuts's vision of Boer and Briton and of black and white living peacefully together and co-operating in building and developing this glorious land of South Africa as the base and the inspiration to all Africa.